Contents

Preface

Part of the stimulus for this book came from working on the DipSW/BA Social Work programme at the North East Wales Institute, where many students undertook assessable practice placements in rural areas. What struck me, was how those who were familiar with rural life usually settled quickly into rural placements, whereas some of those from urban backgrounds struggled to understand how rural communities worked, and sometimes had difficulty in finding an effective way of working. So, I would like to acknowledge the honesty of those who were willing to reveal their uncertainty and their mistakes, and to thank those students and practice teachers from rural backgrounds who were willing to discuss their ideas, even when these seemed to them to be perfectly obvious.

Thanks are due also to several people and organisations who provided useful source information and were happy to respond to my queries: Roy Johnson at Alcohol Concern, Grahame James at Shropshire Social Services, Sally Vaughan at the Save the Children project in Llandrindod Wells, several very committed and helpful workers from Women's Aid groups in Wales and Scotland, and the diligent civil servants at the Scottish Executive and The Office of the National Assembly of Wales. I am also grateful for the comments and support of my colleagues at NEWI, John Bates, Lester Parrott and Debbie Williams, and from Ian Shaw at Cardiff University. However, to spare them any embarrassment or the necessity of having to disassociate themselves from the content of the book, it should be noted that none of them read the whole text, and so any errors and opinions are all my own work.

Finally, thanks to Geoffrey Mann at Russell House, who was willing to let this book increase in length by more than half as much as my original proposal, and to Bridgett Pugh, who once again has been extraordinarily patient with the monomaniacal effort that is required to finish writing any book.

Introduction

This book is about planning and delivering services in a rural context. It is intended primarily for students and practitioners who are beginning work in the countryside, but experienced practitioners may find it useful too. For it might remind them, that much of what seems like 'common-sense' now, was far from obvious when they first began to practice in a rural context. Familiarity and experience tend to give a 'taken-for-granted' quality to much of our knowledge in social work, and sometimes leads practitioners to undervalue their own expertise. This book aims to make explicit some of this 'common-sense' and to help readers develop a more informed understanding of social work in a rural context. An understanding which does not oversimplify the complexity of country life. Although the book focuses upon social work, much of the material about the context, planning and delivery of services is relevant to those who work in other professional services such as health care, and youth and community work, and also to those in voluntary associations who provide counselling, support, advocacy and advice services in rural areas.

Most social work literature and training is written or delivered with the implicit assumption of an urban setting. It operates rather like the default setting on a computer, in that it requires workers to consciously select another setting. That is, to choose to remember that large numbers of British people still live in comparatively rural settings, but unfortunately for those who select the 'rural' option, they are not well-supported by a readily accessible literature, nor for the most part, will their formal training adequately equip them for rural practice. This unconscious and unwitting assumption of a particular type of 'normality' is a persistent feature of discriminatory practice, and can be seen for example, when social work authors write as if not only the clientele is white, but as if all of the readers are too! A further difficulty, and one that is evident whenever social workers attempt to understand the nature of various forms of social differentiation, is that in attempting to gain a better understanding of the life experience of different groups, it is very easy to forget that what is true for the group is

1

not necessarily true for every individual within it. The complexity of individual social location in which many dimensions of potential difference operate, such as age, class, gender, ethnicity, sexuality and so on, means that we should be wary of over-deterministic generalisations about people's situations. Consequently, this book attempts to provide useful general material which can help the reader to appreciate the general context and trends of rural life, without suggesting that these features are necessarily present in every particular situation.

In many respects, social work in the countryside is not essentially different from social work in towns and cities. Indeed, many of the problems which beset people in urban contexts, such as ageism, poverty, illness, disability, child care, racism, sexism, and so on, are also problematic in rural lives. But there are particular features of the rural context that are different, and these influence how people experience their problems and how agencies might need to respond to them. Some of these features are obvious, for example, the geographical spread of the rural population has implications for our efforts to plan and deliver services over large areas. But other features are not so readily apparent because they arise from the different sociological environment of the countryside. While few service users in urban areas would expect to know their social workers, in terms of where they live, their marital status, whether they have children, and who they are related to, in rural areas, such information may be an important feature in establishing the relationship between the worker and the client. As we shall see later in the book, the desire to 'place' people is an enduring feature of rural social relations and one that needs to be negotiated appropriately in order to promote the trust and confidence necessary for effective social work. Indeed, even those whose social work practice is situated entirely in an urban setting, might find that the attempts in this book to describe the general context and dynamics of rural life, through the contrast that it provides with their own setting, actually highlights some of the significant features of their own context.

This book focuses upon social work, because although there is a comprehensive literature addressing community development in rural areas, there is no general equivalent which focuses upon personal social services. Despite several attempts to reshape personal social services into adopting a more proactive role, one which might pre-empt or preclude the need for direct social services to some degree, British statutory authorities have usually isolated personal social services from any efforts that might be made towards enhancing community development, by organisationally separating community development into a different department, often located within youth work and education services rather than social services. The difference between these two approaches is evident in this quotation:

Community development is a way of working which seeks to do two things. First it seeks to release the potential within communities ... Second it works ... to change the relationship between people in communities and the institutions which shape their lives.

(Ronnsby, cited in Moseley, 1997, pp197–8)

In contrast, the personal social services tend to be more 'problem-focused', being primarily concerned with the promotion and development of services geared to the needs of individuals, families and particular groups. While this book recognises the reality of this organisational split, it does not preclude the possibility nor the desirability of changes to the ways in which most social services are delivered. In fact, as the discussion on particular issues such as racism and user involvement demonstrates, the success or failure of initiatives is often dependent upon some element of community education and requires an engagement with the wider community, and there is little doubt that successful rural practice requires a developed appreciation of the ways in which communities work.

Despite the contemporary reframing of many problems as *social exclusion*, a term which offers the possibility of some depathologising of personal problems, I am sceptical about whether this will bring about a more comprehensive and co-ordinated response to social problems. Indeed, as Peters suggests:

... an uncritical acceptance of the normative ideal of 'inclusion' ... can encourage a somewhat totalitarian social strategy, making it impossible to call into question the form of life to which 'inclusion' is sought.

(cited in Pugh and Thompson, 1999, p22)

I suspect that social inclusion will come to be defined very narrowly in terms of participation in work, and as we have seen previously in British welfare policy, when work becomes the primary criterion of who is deserving or undeserving, then those who cannot work may be scapegoated, stigmatised or devalued, and their personal and social needs marginalised. Consequently, this book takes a pragmatic position in regard to contemporary roles and responsibilities and attempts to provide useful information for those seeking to develop current services, while recognising that social workers may need to be wary of the authoritarian implications of some of the more extreme versions of communitarianism and social inclusion.

There are three inter-linked obstacles to developing an understanding of the context of rural lives. Which are, the:

- prevalence of myths and stereotypes about rural life
- complexity of the social and economic situation in rural areas

- absence of accessible and comprehensive information about the rural context

The countryside has always been a canvas upon which people have painted their images of rural life. Sometimes these are presented positively, in bucolic images of rural bliss and in the most extreme image, the countryside is depicted as a haven of simplicity and serenity where life is somehow more natural and real. The idealisation of the countryside ranges from an appreciation of the assumed honesty and earthiness of country folk, through to images of the country cottage as a rural retreat from the stresses and strains of city living. Occasionally this idealisation is reversed, and the same features viewed more negatively. In this alternative picture, simplicity becomes a lack of sophistication, and peace becomes isolation. The virtues of country life become problematic as the interdependence of family life is reinterpreted as an introverted and abusive environment, and neighbourly interest becomes seen as nosiness and gossip. These stereotypical ideas persist partly because of a lack of accurate information about country life. For example, the common assumption of an 'empty' countryside which is becoming further depopulated, leaving behind a stranded, ageing, and increasingly poor populace, is mistaken. As we shall see in Part 1, the reality of contemporary life in the countryside is a great deal more complex than some of these over-simplistic assumptions convey. Unlike people in many other European countries such as France, most people in Britain have little contact with rural life, and are often several generations removed from direct experience of life in the countryside.

Good practice is dependent upon reliable and accurate information, but unfortunately, while there is an extensive literature in the form of reports and pamphlets which is potentially useful for practitioners and policy makers working in rural contexts, most of it is not easily accessible. Much of this material is produced by small groups and regional organisations and rarely surfaces outside of the contexts in which it is published. Consequently, it can be difficult to identify and access this information, much of which has a limited shelf-life anyway. Furthermore, because it often focuses upon a limited range of single-issue topics, typically pre-school provision, poverty, and health care, it rarely considers some of the central features of personal social services work, such as child protection, mental health, and disability, and rarely provides a more general overview of the rural scene. Unfortunately, what social work literature there is on rural life, tends to follow the single-issue approach and is notable for the lack of any broader professional or theoretical perspectives. So, while reference may be made to say, racism or male violence, such issues tend to be addressed in isolation. Much of this material is valuable for its particular purpose, but it is difficult for the beginning practitioner or student to develop any sense of the broader picture. This book attempts to draw together a wide range of information, including source material from rural sociology and geography that would not normally come to the attention of social workers, to help them develop a more comprehensive appreciation of what social work in a rural context entails.

Social work is not a neutral activity, implicitly or explicitly, it is informed by assumptions about how societies and people 'work', and its statutory remit often embodies assumptions about how people should live and behave. Consequently, this book attempts to set the practice of rural social work within the developing perspectives of anti-discriminatory and anti-oppressive practice. Thus, there are six crucial elements derived from these perspectives which underpin this text. They are:

- The recognition of socially structured forms of disadvantage based upon factors such as age, disability, ethnicity, gender, and sexuality.
- A commitment to a value base which encompasses notions of social justice and equality.
- An awareness that professional interventions do not always have beneficial consequences. Thus, social workers' interventions and the assumptions upon which they are based, instead of being solutions in themselves, might actually further compound the difficulties faced by those whom they seek to help.
- A commitment to the development of a needs-led approach to the provision of service. That is, one in which service providers attempt to be responsive to the particular problems of the client, rather than one in which the client simply has to accept what is available.
- A commitment to the empowerment of clients through enhancing their participation in the processes of assessment, planning, implementation and decision making.
- A recognition that all human service work is, explicitly or implicitly, a political activity. That is, an activity which either reinforces and reiterates existing social structures, or alternatively, challenges them.

The structure of the book is simple. Part 1 reviews a wide range of sources to help readers develop an understanding of what is meant by the phrase—'the rural context'. It looks at the various geographic, demographic, social and economic factors that shape life in the countryside and presents a complex and multifaceted picture of the rural context. A context in which issues such as discrimination and disadvantage are presented as important aspects of rural life and not simply as marginal concerns. In some instances, there is a wealth of relevant material, but in others, the published literature in regard to particular issues and rurality is scarce. Thus, while I have tried to address most of the major dimensions of discrimination, some aspects are inevitably less comprehensively referenced.

Part 2 looks at how services are planned and developed from broad general policies instituted by central government through to regional fora and local initiatives. It begins with a brief review of the political context of rural life, and identifies some of the advisory bodies and non-government agencies who contribute to the social and policy context of rural work. It reviews recent policy developments, identifies useful sources of information and data which can be used to support planning and development, and considers the case for a rural premium in the funding allocations made to rural services. Part 2 then goes on to indicate how users and workers may exert influence upon decision making bodies and processes, and finally, it reviews the practicalities and pitfalls of joint working and working with voluntary agencies, pointing up some important issues in work force support, and the evaluation of services.

Part 3 focuses upon practical issues in the delivery of rural social services. It reports relevant research, describes useful innovations, and identifies some of the persistent problems which face service users and providers. It begins by helping workers to understand how and why they need to become socially skilled in their work in rural areas, and then reviews particular services—services to children and families, community care, and services to travellers—and then considers the response to particular issues, such as youth homelessness, racism, 'domestic violence', drug misuse, and rural stress or suicide.

Finally, a word about the language used in this book. I have avoided using masculine pronouns, such as he and his, as generic for both men and women, but where they occur in quotations I have left them as they stand, though they are marked (sic). When referring to a single person I have used the plural forms they and their, because these are easily recognised and their meaning generally understood. Similarly, I have avoided the use of collective nouns, such as mankind, which use maleness as the dominant representation for all people. The use of words like black or blind to convey negative connotations about people and things has also been avoided, and they are only used in their descriptive contexts. The question of how to refer to the people who use our services is a tricky one, for these words are not neutral, and they carry certain connotations about the status of the person who is receiving, in relation to the person who is providing the service. Service user is probably the term most commonly used today and my writing reflects this, but client is also used, partly for variation to avoid over use of the term service user, and partly because for me it still signals a relationship of respect.

Part 1: The Rural Context

Historically, there have been many conflicting and contradictory views about the countryside. Different ideas about rurality have reflected different ideas about the beauty and worth of the countryside, and about the lives of those who live there. For example, Marx and Engels writing in the 1870s were unequivocal in seeing it as a place of oppression, grinding poverty and ignorance. Consequently, they welcomed the urbanising effects of capitalism which:

> ... has created enormous cities, has greatly increased the urban population as compared to the rural, and has thus rescued a considerable part of the population from the idiocy of rural life.
>
> (Marx and Engels, 1972, p36)

The reference to *idiocy* made by Marx and Engels is not a comment upon the intellect of rural people, but picks up a much earlier notion derived from the Greeks, of rural dwellers as being beyond the reach of the polis. That is, outside of the mainstream of political life. Ching and Creed (1997), have argued that the rural/urban distinction is one of the important dimensions by which societies define themselves. There is a cultural hierarchy presumed in the words *urbane* and *rustic*, which are often used to indicate the relative levels of sophistication embodied in urban life as opposed to the simplicity of rural life. This ordering is one which validates the apparent superiority of city dwellers. Nonetheless, there is no single or simple view of the desirability or worth of rural life because there have always been contradictory notions about the countryside. Over a hundred years after Marx and Engel's words were written, Newby (1988), pointed out some of the ways in which urban dwellers have subsequently mythologised the countryside. Typically, by seeing it as a largely unchanged and unchanging place, an unspoiled landscape dotted with quiet rural communities, places which are havens of peace and retreat from the pressures of city living. Indeed, the 'empty' spaces, the woods, fields, hills and moor land, have come to be seen as an 'urban playspace' for the leisure activities of city dwellers who may ride, ramble, and study them (Butler, 1998). In contrast to the perceptions of

Marx and Engels, the countryside has now come to be seen as a desirable place to be, at least for some people, or for some of the time. The fact that many cultural representations of the countryside idealise rural life was wittily sent up by Vaughan who commented that:

> *Painters of the rural scene in the 20th century have been notorious for their inability to see pylons and silage towers. 'Discussing the Milk Quota' and 'Artificial Insemination Day' are still, I believe, subjects awaiting their debut at the Royal Academy.*

> (Short, 1992, p4)

This rather selective representation of the countryside not only omits the realities of contemporary rural life, but fails to acknowledge a history which includes the early development of industrial processes in the countryside in the sixteenth and seventeenth centuries, or recognise the bitter class divisions which existed in some areas.

Nevertheless, it would be mistaken to assume that ideas about the countryside and rural life are now settled questions. As we shall see in the later sections, there is fierce competition not only about the use of countryside 'space', but also about the symbolic value attached to the countryside and rural life. Very real differences remain in terms of ideas about how rural life should be lived and about how communities might be preserved or developed.

Changes in the structure of the rural population, evident in the changing social composition of many villages as new residents move into them, have led to conflicts between different ideas about what the countryside should look like. Some new residents, who see it predominantly as a place of stability and peacefulness and do not view it as a site for work other than farming, consequently oppose any proposed changes in land use or economic developments. There can be a 'drawbridge' effect where new housing, new businesses, and new roads, are opposed by incomers. The inward movement of comparatively affluent home owners with particular ideas about what the countryside should be like, not only prevents villages from changing or growing, but can have other far-reaching effects upon local communities. For example, planning restrictions upon new building can lead to localised housing shortages, when house prices and rents rise beyond the reach of other local people. This, in turn, can lead to an increasing polarisation of the socio-economic structure of the community, as the proportion of relatively wealthy incomers increases (Murdoch and Marsden, 1994). The increasing numbers of those who live in the countryside but commute to work in urban areas in their own transport, where they also conduct their personal business and do their shopping, have begun to shape the look of villages and have diluted local demands for the maintenance of local services such as buses, doctors, schools and post offices. Far from being a haven of bucolic bliss, the countryside is the subject of some fiercely contested ideas about who should be in it. Sibley (1997), in a perceptive essay on how public order legislation has been used to confer the status of 'non-belonging' upon Gypsies, New Age Travellers, ravers and hunt saboteurs, shows how these groups are perceived as alien and damaging to the 'sacred' countryside:

Just as idealised and romanticised representations of English (sic) rural landscapes have no place for chicken factories, gravel pits, electricity pylons and council houses, so the representations of rural society have no room for travellers, factory workers, or ethnic minorities. These groups remain invisible in these versions of rural life.

(Sibley, 1997, p228)

While these contested ideas might simply seem to be about space and who uses it, the countryside often has a significant role in constructing ideas of identity and otherness. Therefore, these are not simply struggles about planning laws and public order, they may also represent broader conflicts about the nature of society. Ideas about the countryside can have a powerful symbolic value in representing particular ideas about nationalism, bound-aries and belongingness. Sibley makes the point that in England, the countryside has long been invested with a 'sacred' quality, arising from the notion that it represents the essence of Englishness. Thus, the idealisation of a supposedly unchanging landscape populated by peaceful homogenous communities, may at times be seen to be threatened and 'endangered by the transgressions of discrepant minorities' (1997, p219). However, while ideas about 'Englishness' may be represented through images of the tranquillity of its 'green and pleasant land', we should recognise that all cultural ideas are socially situated. That is, they arise from particular social locations and experiences, and so are unlikely to be shared by all groups within a society, or even be held in similar ways in different countries (Schama, 1995). For example, in their images of their countryside many Welsh people might refer to the rugged hills and mountains, and it is no coincidence that these features represent independence and endurance, and so, aptly for them, stand as symbols of resistance to English economic, cultural and political dominance. By now, it should be beginning to become obvious to the reader, that the apparent simplicity of what we mean by the 'countryside' is deceptive. Different ideas about the countryside represent real differences in perceptions of the nature of society, and the existence of these different ideas undermines any simplistic notions of stability and homogeneity that we

9

might have about the countryside and those who live there. As we shall see later in the discussion of racism, it is not the existence of difference in the countryside that is problematic, but the perception and meanings attached to such difference.

Forming a clear picture of the countryside and what is happening to it is difficult, because as Cloke et al., note, much of what we 'know' about the countryside is a product of what we choose to study (Cloke et al., 1997). Since the 1970s, many studies of rural life have either focused upon continuity and stability, or alternatively, have focused upon conflict and change. Most studies are of particular villages and communities and do not develop any analysis of the meanings attached to the countryside, nor do they analyse its relationship to the rest of society. One common feature of many studies, is that they begin by attempting to define the term 'rural', but later reluctantly conclude that there is no single overall definition. While this is undoubtedly the case, most writers fail to point out what the significance of this problem is. Because most are seeking to establish what might be termed 'technical' definitions, they fail to indicate the sociological signifi-cance of this question of definition. Of course, the plethora of definitions indicates mundane differences of perception, but their problems with the 'slipperiness' of definitions of rurality stem from a failure to understand the symbolic importance of different ideas about the countryside. Nevertheless, while the next section briefly summarises some of the different ways in which rurality can be defined, for the purposes of this book, it is more useful to devote attention to some of the consequences that flow from these different approaches rather than deconstruct the differences of definition.

Francis and Henderson suggest that rural issues can be understood as having two significant, and overlapping, components:

- The broad trends affecting rural areas, e.g. changes in agriculture, the dilution of rural culture.
- The problems affecting people in rural areas, which may have much in common with problems in urban situations, e.g. unemployment, poor housing.

(Francis and Henderson, 1992, p6)

This is a helpful way of beginning to engage with the subject because it starts with a focus upon the general context and then shifts to more specific issues. The remainder of this chapter is broadly structured in this way, with the first sections establishing the wider context of rural life in terms of population trends, economic changes, social networks, rural identity, and so on. The later sections are more problem centred, focusing upon issues such as poverty, discrimination and disadvantage. The distinction made by Francis and Henderson is also useful because it helps to signal a very important point indeed, namely that:

> *We need to recognise how far we are dealing with rural problems per se and how far we are dealing with more general problems which have a particular manifestation in the rural context.*

(Barnes, 1993, p5)

Defining Rural

Clearly, the question of what we mean by 'rurality' is a complex one, and unsurprisingly, many social researchers have spent a great deal of effort in tackling it. Practically, the problems of definition can be avoided by conceptualising a continuum of settlement that runs from low to high density, that is from rural to urban. This, as Robinson (1998), notes, acknowledges that the division between rurality and urbanity is an arbitrary one. That is, that there is no absolute distinction, but instead, a series of choices that we might make about how to define what we consider 'rural'. Choosing between different types of definition might seem to be a rather irrelevant and arcane question, but, because different ways of defining rural emphasise some features or perceptions rather than others, they can have important consequences when policy decisions are being made about social and economic targets, priorities and resources. For example, when the size of the community is used as the defining feature in decisions on health care or education, then other aspects, such as the degree of geographical isolation may be ignored. Yet it may be the distance from another larger centre of population which is the most important factor influencing the ease of access to services for rural dwellers. This issue, and its implications for the planning and development of rural social services is examined further in Part 2.

Barnes (1993), in a useful review of this issue summarised the main distinctions, when she identified four main ways of defining 'rural'. Namely, to:

- Define urban areas first, and then classify the remaining areas as rural.
- Define villages and settlements below a certain population size as rural.
- Identify particular characteristics which are thought to indicate rurality, such as population density, distance from a larger urban centre, or types of economic activity, and apply these to existing administrative divisions such as local authority districts, parishes, electoral wards, and postal districts.
- Ask people and organisations to define themselves.

11

While the first three types of definition represent attempts to provide an objective criterion, the last one is rather different. When we ask people to define for themselves what is 'rural', we come much closer to their subjective perceptions of themselves and their communities. The National Federation of Women's Institutes used this approach in their study entitled *The Changing Village* (1999). They surveyed over eight thousand local Women's Institutes and found that 82.6 per cent of their respondents classified themselves as 'rural', without necessarily defining exactly what they meant by this. Of course, many people in rural areas may not have explicit definitions of rurality, but most will have some implicit notions of what it is. What is most significant is that their definitions will not usually be confined to objective factors such as population characteristics or types of employment, such as forestry or farming. Instead, they will often encompass ideas about social networks and personal identity. Consequently, ideas about place and belonging are crucial elements in understanding the rural context of social services.

The definition of rurality through people's subjective perceptions not only accepts the possibility of different perceptions of the countryside, but also opens up the question of power. What should be recognised is that the process of definition is an act which creates a category within a particular frame of reference and with particular meanings. Murdoch and Pratt have suggested that:

we should be extremely wary of attempts to definitively define the rural ... *[because any definition] ... is saturated with assumptions and presuppositions.*
(1997, p56)

The key word here is 'definitively', that is, the notion that there is some fixed and enduring idea of what is rural. Instead, we have to recognise that all definitions are socially constructed and remind ourselves that there are pertinent questions to be asked, about:

- the nature of the definition
- who is doing the defining
- in what circumstances this is being done
- and to what purpose

For example, while many people would accept that traditional gypsies have a 'place' in the countryside, they are unwilling to extend their acceptance to new age travellers. Such distinctions have considerable import when decisions are being made about the provision of education, health, housing and social services. The crucial point is that we need to be aware that conventional representations and definitions of rural life may portray the countryside as if it were an integrated and organic entity in which conflict, difference and diversity is absent, or is underplayed. Thus, some people's ideas and needs may come to predominate our perceptions to the exclusion of those of other less powerful, less popular, and less visible people. As we shall see later in Part 2, there is an important role for social workers in responding to unmet needs and hearing the 'voice' of those who are otherwise ignored or marginalised.

The Rural Population

Urbanisation, the movement of people from the countryside and the increasing concentration of the population in the cities and towns, began earlier and was more rapid in the British Isles than in most other European countries. In France this shift took place over a much longer period, for example, farm households as a percentage of the overall population fell from 47 per cent in 1962 to 27 per cent in 1982 (Cohen, 1995). During the late 18th century and the early 19th century this population shift was driven by a number of factors. Changes in farming methods and early mechanisation reduced the demand for rural labour, while the enclosures of common land together with reductions in real wages, and legislative changes, reduced the capacity of people to support themselves by subsistence farming, and itinerant labour (Perkin, 1969). Poor Law restrictions made it difficult to undertake seasonal work or to travel easily from parish to parish to supplement family income. The Irish famine of 1845, and the clearances in Scotland, where tenant farmers were driven from the land to make way for more extensive sheep rearing, resulted in depopulation and also stimulated the drift towards the expanding urban areas or to migration overseas. Meanwhile, in the rapidly growing cities and towns the development of new industries and the industrialisation of old methods of production led to an unprecedented increase in the size of the urban population. It would be easy to assume that this phenomenon belongs to the past, but even today, there is a complex pattern of 'push and pull' influences operating upon the much smaller rural population, and the comparatively early urbanisation of the UK has had some enduring effects.

The continuing mechanisation of farming, and the increasing land area needed for economically viable units, together with the growing specialisation of land use since the Second World War has further reduced the demand for rural labour. Thus, in areas without any other economic base, such as quarrying or tourism, there has been a continuing downward pressure upon the numbers living and working in the countryside. This is particularly evident in the more remote areas of the British Isles. Nevertheless, in rural areas closer to other sources of work, or made more accessible by improved road networks, there have been increases in population and especially in the numbers of relatively affluent residents. This process of repopulation has been termed 'counter-urbanisation' and is evident in a number of other countries (Berry, 1976; Champion, 1989). Although many of these 'new' settlers are what Ilbery terms the 'service classes', those who 'work either in the public sector or private economic and social services; they have relatively high incomes, high job security and high educational attainment' (1998, p5), not all of them are so clearly members of this middle class grouping. There is some doubt as to whether the phrase, the 'service classes' actually describes any concrete social reality other than the relative affluence of many incomers, for among these new settlers there may be quite wide disparities in tastes, in political views, and in general lifestyles (Phillips, 1998). It is probably more useful to conceive of the rural middle classes as being a socio-economic group comprised of somewhat disparate elements, whose most common feature may be their comparative wealth or income. Interestingly, a number of researchers have suggested that some elements of the rural middle classes share very similar ideals about the countryside with many so called new age travellers (Hetherington, 1995; Urry, 1995).

Studies into the reasons for moving and the distances moved, suggest that higher income households are more likely to move greater distances than lower income groups and are more likely to be moving because of changes in employment. Lewis and Sherwood (1994), in their study of movements in England, suggested that where people had pre-existing links with an area, they usually had a particular location in mind even before their final decision to move was made. Harper (1991) suggests that while many moves used to be to places where people had some pre-existing links, increasingly it seems to reflect a more general preference for living in the countryside, and thus, it is the availability of housing generally rather than a particular preference for one place that is influential in personal decision making. However, he is careful to point out the complex interaction of factors that influence personal choices, and notes that there are still marked differences across regions. A fuller discussion of trends in counter-urbanisation can be found in the work of Lewis (1998). Finally, even in the more remote areas, some inward movement has partly offset the seemingly inexorable decline in population. The growth in tourism and rural leisure activities has provided some opportunities for work, and there has been some inward movement of those who seek 'alternative' lifestyles.

Population patterns and trends
Though different definitions of what constitutes rurality lead to different estimations of the total number of people living in the countryside, there is

14

no doubt that however it is defined, the number remains surprisingly high, especially given the long history of urbanisation. For example, one estimate suggested that there were around 11.5 million people living in rural areas in the UK, including Northern Ireland (Age Concern, 1998). In contrast, the 1991 Census showed that the rural population of England, Scotland and Wales constituted 10.4 per cent of the total population, a slight increase from the previous census in 1981 at 10.38 per cent, giving a UK total of around 6.1 million people. However, these overall proportions tend to disguise the higher percentages found in the most rural areas of Scotland and Wales—the Western Isles, Orkney, Shetland and Powys—where between 57 per cent and 70 per cent of the local population is classified as living in the countryside. The proportions in the most rural counties in England, Cornwall and Somerset, are respectively 36.1 per cent and 31.4 per cent. In total, there are 24 areas in the UK where more than 20 per cent of the local population lives in the countryside (Denham and White, 1998). Population density measured by persons per square kilometre range from eight in the Highland region of Scotland through to 23 in Powys, the least populous county in England and Wales, through to 60 in Northumberland and a surprising 152 in Devon. The average for Great Britain as a whole is 243 people per square kilometre (Champion and Watkins, 1991).

It is not easy to briefly summarise the complexity of the actual distribution of the rural population, and population numbers and density figures do not adequately convey the physical distribution of the rural population, because there are wide local variations arising from factors like the landscape, local transport networks, affordable housing, access to local services, employment opportunities, and so on. Another way of indicating the broad picture of distribution is to make statements about the number and size of rural communities. For example, Barnes (1993), reported that in England there were over 19,300 villages and hamlets with a population of 3,000 or less. While the general distribution of population is a significant factor in planning and delivering services, as we shall see later, there is no substitute for the detailed analysis of a particular locality.

In general, the rural population reflects the broad trends evident throughout the rest of the UK population, for example, increased divorce rates, smaller families with fewer children, but there are some points of difference. The proportion of young children up to four years of age is smaller than in urban areas, and there is a smaller proportion of young adults between 18 and 29 years of age. While this latter group constitutes 18.7 per cent of the population in English urban areas, they comprise only 14.6 per cent in rural areas. For those aged over 75 years, the typical pattern is of a slightly higher proportion of older men in rural areas compared to urban areas, and a slightly lower proportion of older women (Denham and White, 1998). Of course, these overall figures again mask more marked variations in particular localities, and in communities with declining employment opportunities, or those that are popular destinations for retirement, there are typically much higher proportions of older people. For example, in Dorset, 35 per cent of the population is over 65 compared to a UK average of around 19 per cent (Warnes and Ford, 1993).

While the degree of ethnic and 'race' diversity in rural areas is generally lower than in most urban areas, every area of the UK has some minority ethnic population within it. In the predominantly rural counties of England, the proportion of residents who were born outside of the UK ranges from 0.9 per cent in Northumbria, through 1.8 per cent in Devon, to 7.4 per cent in Leicestershire (Rickford, 1995). Furthermore, these figures severely underestimate ethnic diversity because they do not include those people from ethnic minorities who were born within the UK, nor do they include the British born children of overseas born residents. The 1991 Census indicates that for just one group, that is those describing themselves as 'Afro-Caribbean', there were over 33,000 people living in small villages and the wider countryside (Office of Population Censuses and Surveys, 1992). Jay (1992), estimated that there were between 26,200 and 36,600 people who might be perceived as black living in south-west England, that is, Cornwall, Devon, Dorset and Somerset. Interestingly, there are distinct differences between rural and urban areas in the patterns of settlement of different minority ethnic groups:

Whereas there is no significant difference overall between the proportions of the ethnic minority groups in urban and rural areas who are Black (30.0 per cent and 29 per cent respectively), the proportion of (ethnic minorities) who are Indians, Pakistanis and Bangladeshis in urban areas (49.3 per cent), is almost double that of rural areas (25 per cent). And for Chinese the situation is reversed, with just 4.9 per cent of the total ethnic minority population in urban areas belonging to this group compared with 7.8 per cent . . . in rural parts of the country.

(Denham and White, 1998, p30)

While the specific reasons for these variations are not conclusively identified, the likely factors are employment opportunities, the availability of affordable housing, social links to pre-existing settlements, local facilities, and English language competency. It will be interesting to see whether recent changes in policies on the acceptance and settlement of refugees, with increased access and a return to policies of dispersal, will in the longer term become evident in these statistics. The age profile of the ethnic minority population is younger than the predominant 'white' majority, with a higher proportion of children under 5 years, and young people from 5–19 years. Conversely, there are much lower proportions of ethnic minority older people in the age groups 60–74, and 75 and over. While 7 per cent of the 'white' population is over 75, only 0.7 per cent of the ethnic minority population is in this age band (Population Trends, 88, Summer 1997, p23).

The social class composition of rural areas is different from urban areas, particularly in England and Wales, where there is a higher proportion of 'heads of household' in social classes I and II (professional and managerial occupations). This is most marked in social class II. In Wales, for example, only 14 per cent of those in urban areas are in this category compared to 23.5 per cent in rural areas (1991 Census). Consequently, while there is some historical basis for the myth of rural depopulation, the actual demography of the countryside is rather more complex. As noted in the previous section, there is a well-established process of counter-urbanisation occurring and, far from becoming an emptier place, overall numbers are increasing and the composition of this population is changing in terms of income, social class, and lifestyle (Champion, 1989).

Finally, one point is worth noting, which is how stable patterns of population have remained in some areas, particularly those where the economic base has been relatively constant, and this is especially evident in areas where small farms have continued to exist. The consequences of this for patterns of settlement and family life can be seen in the experience of two south Shropshire sisters. In an interview with their local paper in which they reflected on their lives, Nellie, aged 85, had never lived anywhere else, and Mollie, 91, had never moved very far and she had eleven children, all of whom lived locally except for one son who had moved about 12 miles away (Eldon Lee, 1999).

The Rural Economy

Farming is often seen as the main economic activity in rural areas, but it is a mistake to think of the rural economy solely in terms of agriculture. There are other traditional industries which are important sources of employment, such as quarrying, forestry, and mining, as well as work in the utility companies supplying water, electricity and telecommunications, and also a significant number of jobs in the various public services. Over the last twenty years there has been a marked trend towards the ruralisation of industry, and, as a result, the proportion of the rural work force who are employed in manufacturing industry is only slightly lower than the national average (Champion and Watkins, 1991). This trend is sometimes referred to as a shift from urban to rural, but in most instances firms have not relocated, instead the trend is due to the comparatively stronger growth of rural industry compared to that in urban areas (North, 1998). Another notable feature of change in rural areas over the last century has been the decline in jobs in private service in the larger country houses, which had formerly been a major source of employment for both men and women. Nevertheless, agriculture, along with its associated industries such as food processing, including dairies and creameries, packing and canning, abattoirs, livestock services, haulage, seed and feed stock merchants, agricultural machinery and farm suppliers, remains a significant source of employment in rural areas. Farming, however, is undergoing profound changes in the way that it is organised, in the types and levels of production, and particularly in its relationship to market forces (Ilbery, 1998). Consequently, the longer term decline of employment opportunities in British agriculture has been exacerbated over the last twenty years by further mechanisation and the increased industrialisation of farming practices on the larger farms, accompanied by declining incomes on smaller owner-occupied and rented farms who continue to struggle 'to compete on increasingly unfavourable terms or are severely handicapped by their limited scale of operations' (Champion and Watkins, 1991, p10). One government survey cited by Champion and Watkins found that only 28 per cent of farms employed any workers other than the manager/owner, thus, most small holdings rely entirely upon the labour of a single person, perhaps supported by a partner, with some using contractors for jobs they cannot manage alone (MAFF, 1989). While mechanisation has been a major cause of the reduction in jobs, many workers also left the industry voluntarily, often because of low wages.

The most dramatic change in the rural economy has been the massive reduction in the agricultural workforce, which has diminished by some 60,000 farming jobs over the last ten years (Hetherington, 1999). Today, less than 2.1 per cent of men and less than 0.6 per cent of women are formally employed in the main rural industries—agriculture, hunting, forestry and fishing (Regional Trends, 1998). The total of employees in the UK, not including self-employed workers, involved in agriculture, hunting and forestry was approximately 266,000 in 1998 (Annual Abstract of Statistics, 1999). Even the inclusion of small farms where people are self employed does not raise the overall figure above 4 per cent of the total workforce. In comparison, in the EU generally, agricultural employment fell from 21 per cent of the economically active population in 1962 to 7 per cent in 1992 (Cohen, 1995). One interesting aspect of farm work is that for most labourers it is not a permanent job but, often a period of employment early in their working careers from which they move on to other work (Champion and Watkins, 1991). Seasonal and casualised work is still a notable feature of rural employment, and in 1997 there were 154,400 regular workers in agriculture and 80,900 seasonal or casual workers (Annual Abstract of Statistics, 1999). While a full explanation of the possible reasons for the changes in rural employment are beyond the scope of this book, it is worth noting the main factors in regard to farming are: the loss of export markets due to the BSE ban on beef exports; the high level of the pound; declining levels of agricultural subsidies; high levels of debt; the expanded common market of the European Community; changes in consumer preferences; and, the increased power of large food retailers to squeeze producers' profit margins. Consequently, incomes for some farmers have declined dramatically, in some cases to a quarter of their former levels, and many are struggling to keep going. Amongst the hardest hit are small hill farmers, like Les in Cumbria who said:

We've hung on and done everything we've been asked to do. We're only here through the grace of the banks. Politicians talk about diversifying into other areas but this area's so remote there's nothing else I can do. The only option is doing contract work for other farmers.

(Cook, 1999, p15)

There are of course, considerable variations in income between the richest and the poorest farmers, and for those whose farming could not sustain them fully, diversification into other activities such as contracting, including ploughing, harvesting, hedge cutting and so on, haulage, landscaping, farm shops, golf courses, caravan sites, bed and breakfast and holiday rentals, has been a common response to declining income. However, this is not a new development as many farmers on smallholdings have long had to supplement their incomes by undertaking other work off the farm. Cloke et al. (1997), found that many had other jobs and farmed in the evenings and at weekends, while their wives ran the home and replaced their labour during the day. Nevertheless, declining farm incomes and reduced employment, together with some of the other changes in population and developments in retailing, particularly the spread of large supermarkets at the edges of many rural towns, has led to marked changes in many villages. Over the past decade, more than 1,000 village shops have closed, along with nearly 500 post offices. The result, as the National Federation of Women's Institute survey (1999), indicated, was that 30 per cent of villages had no shop and that post office closures were continuing.

One feature of the countryside which is often overlooked is the existence of small industrial villages. Typically, these were centred around a single source of employment, such as mining, and many of these have subsequently declined as employment opportunities diminished. Where there has been a more diverse economic base, and particularly where there have been developments in food processing and timber products, such villages remain important centres of activity. Interestingly, the lack of economic diversity is often reflected in the social structure of such villages which are often predominantly unskilled, semi-skilled or working class communities. Such communities may be economically vulnerable because of their dependence upon one or two relatively large employers, and can be small pockets of deprivation amongst otherwise comfortable areas, as their residents have few alternative sources of employment, low incomes, few financial resources, and relatively low levels of education and qualifications. Home working, that is working under contract or for oneself in one's own home, is widespread, generally being three times as common in rural areas than in towns. But there are regional variations, and home workers, 'in rural Wales, in fact . . . were more than five times as common, and in rural Scotland, ten times' (Denham and White, 1998, p34).

Another consequence of the economic decline of agriculture has been increased pressure to allow other forms of land use. Government policy, which since the Second World War has been predominantly geared to food production, is now being reviewed. As well as the recognition of the increasingly significant development of tourism, there is pressure to release more land for house building and to relax planning restrictions on alternative uses for farm buildings. The role of the regional development agencies in helping to regenerate other forms of activity and employment have been quite significant in some areas of the UK, and in some places have led to significant population growth. However, this 'economic marginality' can also be exploited by companies seeking to site polluting, dangerous and other sensitive operations in areas where there is a potentially grateful and compliant work force and the likelihood of sympathetic consideration of planning permission and possible financial assistance from local and regional government bodies (Cloke et al., 1997). Such developments include chemical works, wind farms, nuclear establishments, expanded quarrying, weapons and arms dumps, refuse disposal and landfill, and power stations. Often, proposals for development result in a political division in a community between those who stand to gain, like potential employees and landowners, and those who wish to 'preserve' the countryside. Such divisions often reflect the interplay of different class interests and perceptions of who and what the countryside is 'for' (Murdoch and Marsden, 1994).

Transport

There have been many studies of rural transport and most have focused upon the decline in public transport and the increasing dependency upon private motoring (Lowe, Bradley and Wright, 1986; McLaughlin, 1986).

While car ownership rates are very high in rural areas, averaging between 70 and 80 per cent of households, there are still substantial numbers of people who have no access to a private motor car (Denham and White, 1998). The increasing dependency upon the motor car has also resulted from changing patterns in the provision of commercial and public services. The decline in local schools, shops, post offices, churches and pubs has necessitated longer journeys to access them. The reduction of local services impacts differently upon people according to whether or not they need them. Thus, it is the elderly, those on low incomes, mothers with young children and people with disabilities who are most likely to face transport difficulties (Buchanan, 1983; Gant and Smith, 1991). The central theme that has emerged from these studies is that lack of transport is both a cause and a consequence of rural deprivation (Shaw, 1979). Consequently, households with low incomes in areas with poor transport networks and with widely dispersed services and jobs are more vulnerable to a self-reinforcing position of deprivation. For example, Cloke et al. (1994), found that 61 per cent of women and 39 per cent of men in their English study area had difficulty finding suitable employment and that transport difficulties were a significant factor in this problem. Moreover, there are marked differences in the extent to which men and women were able to drive and had access to private transport. Even when women did have access to a car, this was often limited to times when their partners were not using it to get to work themselves, or to when their partner could take them. Furthermore, a later study in rural Wales by Cloke et al. (1997) found that the differences in access between different households and between men and women varied quite sharply from one district to another.

Government transport policies over the past 20 years have been inconsistent and somewhat erratic in regard to rural services. Public subsidy of school bussing has declined and while some subsidies for ordinary bus routes still exist, the deregulation of the bus services following the 1985 Transport Act, which was intended to encourage competition and improve services, has not generally improved matters. Increases in fuel taxes and Road Fund Licences have hit harder in the countryside than in the towns, not simply because people are more reliant upon private transport, but also because many relatively poor car owners might be seen as reluctant owners. That is, their car represents a disproportionate drain upon their household income, which their urban counterparts might not have to contend with. Palmer's research in Scotland suggests 'that car ownership is correlated more with remoteness than household prosperity (and) in turn, the outlay on purchase, maintenance and running costs may well prejudice other aspects of quality of life' (Palmer, 1991, p96). However, while some groups have difficulties, it is also the case that many rural people do not have difficulties in gaining access to services. A significant proportion of households have two cars and do not experience their relative isolation from services as being problematic (Cloke et al., 1997). Where people have strong social networks they are often able to mitigate some of the worst effects of lack of transport with the help of other people, who may provide lifts, fetch shopping, and make time and space for them to access employment or services, by child minding, looking after livestock, and so on.

Transport is also a problem for those delivering services, either because of the increased costs incurred in providing domiciliary or dispersed services, or because it militates against the recruitment of suitably located staff. This is especially the case in home care services, where wages are low and where staff are less likely to have their own transport. As the Social Services Inspectorate (SSI) found when they visited Dorset, 'One person exemplified the problem. She told us that without a car she could leave the village on a Monday morning to go to work, but could not return until Thursday evening if reliant on public transport!' (SSI, 1999, p22). Furthermore, the vagaries of the weather have a greater impact in rural areas and create problems in the more remote and hilly districts. Some workers, nonetheless, make great efforts to meet their commitments, as the same inspectors noted, 'we were told of home carers who had, during bad weather conditions reached their visit on horseback as it had been impossible by car' (SSI, 1999, p21).

Community and Identity

While sociologists and geographers may debate whether the concept of community has much analytical value, or prefer to use notions of system and network analysis (Russell, 1975), it nonetheless remains an idea that people perceive as having meaning. It is sometimes assumed that a community shares a common world view and a common set of norms, but Rapport in his study of a Cumbrian village found that although there were 'many communal forms of behaviour . . . (there was no) standard definition of what these would entail among the inhabitants' of the village (Sibley, 1997, p64) An alternative way of approaching the issue of community is to focus on how and where the boundaries of community are established in people's minds. As Durkheim pointed out in 1897, a sense of social solidarity can be maintained by the drawing of boundaries, and by the identification and exclusion of those who transgress them, or are otherwise perceived as a threat to the community (Giddens, 1978). For example, Murdoch and Marsden, whilst undertaking some research into rural life in Buckinghamshire, recorded their experience of being confronted as unknown strangers in a small community:

Driving into a picturesque, self-contained, affluent village we were immediately struck by how visible we were. The few people on the street stopped to regard us with quiet intent as we were, of course, strangers. We were in the village to interview the local vicar and this was our first experience of fieldwork in this particular place ... Having located the vicarage ... we pulled into the driveway, got out of the car and rang the doorbell. There was no reply, so we waited for a couple of minutes and rang the doorbell again, but at that moment a large estate car pulled very sharply into the drive and a middle-aged woman jumped out, demanding to know what we wanted. The vicar apparently no longer lived in the vicarage, but in a new bungalow further down the street. The woman brusquely told us how to find his house and waited for us to leave. By this time our feeling of visibility had become extremely acute. Clearly, this woman had not returned home fortuitously at that point and coincidentally, she had known that there were two strangers standing at her front door. Quite how she had been alerted so quickly remained a mystery to us.

(Murdoch and Marsden, 1994, pv)

This experience of informal surveillance in rural areas is hardly unique, and though it might not always represent the style of interaction adopted by insiders to strangers, which in this case may be seen as a very confident middle-class challenge to their presence, it is indicative of how networks can operate to maintain the boundaries and security of a community. Given the contemporary hysteria and negative views commonly expressed about travellers and gypsies, it would be easy to assume that country folk have been, and always are, suspicious of outsiders. Indeed, as Sibley has suggested, the extent to which communities need to assert their boundaries may well be a reflection of the sense of security that they feel. Thus, while outsiders are often received with suspicion and hostility, this is not an inevitable response. Wenger reports the recollections of Mrs Johnson, a Welsh speaking country woman who lived all her life in and around the small village in which she had been born in 1899:

She was conscious of having worked hard and being a good and tolerant neighbour. She continued to take pride in her friendly interactions long ago with tramps and gypsies who were common in the area in her early years

(Wenger, 1994, p67).

Perhaps her perspective reflected the self-confidence and security of a stable community in those days? Of course, in the past, many itinerants were welcomed as seasonal workers, and increased contact and familiarity tends to undermine the more lurid forms of demonisation. In Murdoch and

Marsden's example, the likely perception was that they might have been housebreakers or con men!

Nevertheless, the security of identity reflects to some degree the sense of economic and social security that people feel, and it is interesting to see how the post-war acceptance of the idea that agriculture was, and legitimately so, the dominant force in the countryside has been eroded. No longer is agriculture perceived as a benevolent and benign force. Changes in subsidies and price support arrangements, an increased scepticism about the effects of intensive farming and prairie production, and more recently, extreme distrust about the risks of genetically modified crops and animals, have changed the social environment in which farmers see themselves. Consequently, British farmers have begun:

... to feel, and indeed, to experience an increasing sense of insecurity and uncertainty as regards their position in both agriculture and rural life generally.

(Halfacree, 1997, p71)

and this, to some degree, mirrors the situation before the last war when British agriculture was in a very precarious state. After some thirty years of relative security, from the 1950s to the mid 1980s, when the government tried to maximise farm output, the goal has shifted towards reducing output (Ilbery, 1998). As Giddens (1991), has noted, the sense that things are changing fast, that stability is disappearing, erodes the personal sense of certainty not only in terms of one's self-identity, but also in the reliability of social arrangements, people, and things. Although there is some doubt about whether suicides among farmers have increased in recent years, many commentators have referred to the increasing economic insecurity experienced by farmers and also to the sense that their world is changing in ways that some of them find hard to cope with. In conditions of ontological insecurity, that is, situations where individuals feel insecure in their ideas about themselves and their place in the world, another alternative response is to become more active in reducing the sense of risk. For example, fear of rural crime can lead to increased surveillance through initiatives such as 'Farm Watch', and greater patrolling of the boundaries of rural life.

The important point is that the degree to which communities assert their boundaries and display intolerance of outsiders, or even of the behaviour of people considered to be part of the community itself, is not fixed. It is arguable that during the 1960s and the 1970s the predecessors of today's New Age travellers were not perceived as being so much of a threat as they are today. Nevertheless, it has often been the case that country people have perceived urban areas as the source of threats to their security:

Working-class plotland dwellers in the 1920s, newly mobile motorists and motor cyclists in the 1930s, New Age travellers, ravers and hunt saboteurs in the 1990s have all been represented by antagonists as deviant groups of urban origin.

(Sibley, 1997, p220)

In his theory of structuration, Giddens has argued that social conceptions such as gender and class are not fixed entities, but rather are social constructions created and reiterated through human action (1984). Therefore, they continue to be significant aspects of social life, because in their everyday lives people think and act as if they are real and concrete things. Arguably, communities are constructed in the same way, for it is not necessarily a fact that they are homogeneous and socially coherent entities, but it may well be a fact that people believe them to be so. Consequently, because community is a construct that has to be enacted and represented through a multitude of social interactions, there is always fluidity and some potential for change in any community. Murdoch and Pratt suggest that this is apparent in the ways in which there is often a disparity between a community's notions about itself and how its members should behave, and the acceptance of idiosyncratic and unconformist behaviour by some of its members (1997). Of course, the critical point is whether particular behaviour is tolerated more when the person displaying it is already perceived to be a member. It can be useful to consider two processes, affiliation and differentiation, which operate to establish the particular notions that people have about their communities. First, people may attempt to show how their community differs from other rural or urban areas, the act of differentiation. Second, they may identify what they see as the common or shared features of their community, the act of affiliation. Therefore, tolerance of personal idiosyncrasies may arise from a positive overall balance in these two processes. An individual may be regarded as an 'awkward cuss', but nevertheless remains an insider because they are perceived as being not like other outsiders, or perceived as being more like other insiders than other outsiders. The characteristics that are valued and devalued may be wholly individualised, but can also have a more general social currency, so that having a particular occupation, or family connection, or the capacity to speak a valued language in an area, may offset other negatively perceived aspects of a person's behaviour.

We should not assume that there is any necessary coherence in the identity or identities within a community. For example, Wales may seem to the:

... rest of the world (to be) a coherent picture of cultural self-sufficiency and a firm sense of identity. What outsiders see, however, is not so much Wales as their own reflection, or stereotypes of Welshness ... As one begins to penetrate

*beyond this refracted image . . . One is left not so much with a coherent notion of
Welshness . . . as with a sense of many conflicting and interlocking definitions of
identity which actively compete for symbolic space and public recognition.*
(Bowie, cited in Murdoch and Pratt, 1997, p64)

So the sense in which people are, or expect to be, embedded within
particular communities is in part a reflection of expectations, and where
these are highly idealised there may be a considerable gulf between the
image and the reality.

Belonging and the importance of 'place'

There are two aspects to the notion of 'place'. First, it refers to the
geographical sense of an area or locality that people hold in their minds, and
second, to a social landscape which exists within the physical terrain. This
'sense of a place' is a subjective phenomenon which varies according to
individual perceptions of space, boundaries, insiders and outsiders, social
roles, and social networks. The idea of place extends from ideas about what
is 'home' and what it should look like, through to ideas about social
significance, that is, the relative significance of different people in a person's
social landscape. It is common for people in rural areas to have much higher
expectations in terms of the information they 'need' about other people
whom they are going to engage with in some way. However, caution is
necessary because, as one man told me, 'You've got to be careful, you're a
long time living with your mistakes in the country'. This wariness indicates
the understanding that in small, relatively stable communities, the behaviour
of other people, as well as their presence, is potentially more intrusive.

In rural areas, the social and psychological terrain that is encompassed as
familiar territory in the minds of those who live there tends to be much
greater than in urban areas, and so it is often difficult to ignore the actions
of other people in the same way as in towns and cities. Unlike urban areas,
where notions of what is considered private, semi-private, familiar and safe
space, and may only extend over part of an area, perhaps one or two streets
or not even, in some instances, beyond one's front door, country people
typically perceive a much more extensive area as 'home ground'. Of course,
this doesn't mean that they personally own or control this territory, but it is
the space that is familiar and predictable to them. These ideas make up the
subjective social and physical geographies of an area which are held by the
people who live within it. They are mental maps not only of the terrain, but
also of the people who occupy it. These geographies represent different
expectations about how people should behave, especially in terms of such
things as courtesy, gossip, privacy, participation, reciprocity, and so on.

A failure to understand this larger conception of territory and some of the complex ways in which it is constructed results in a lack of appreciation of the mental landscape of country people and the meanings it holds for them. Some commentators on rural life seem to find it difficult to understand how a farmer whose agricultural practices they may dislike, can apparently be so concerned by the seemingly minor actions of other people and groups elsewhere. What they fail to appreciate, is that many farmers may reluctantly accept what they have to do on their own land as a matter of economic necessity, but regard other local areas as stable and unchanging features of the landscape. Furthermore, because many understand that what is regarded as 'natural', is, in fact, a product of human intervention, and having direct knowledge about how landscapes can be altered, amended and restored, they realise that most of their actions are, in the larger scale of events, transient and temporary in their effects. Even the efforts of conservation groups to 'improve' the countryside may be regarded with mixed feelings by locals, whose responses may range from acceptance, through amusement, to outright hostility. One farmer, observing conservationists cutting down coniferous trees within a mixed deciduous wood, commented that it showed their ignorance of wildlife, since where would the smaller birds now shelter in winter from the weather and larger predatory birds? In this instance, this view of the intrusion and the ineptness of interfering outsiders was further confirmed, when the conservationists accidentally set fire to the woods as they burned the cuttings!

Insiders and outsiders

Champion and Watkins have pointed out that while the notion of conflict between incomers and locals is a recurring theme in images of country life which has some substance, 'there is no simple division between incomer and local' (1991, p15), and it is a mistake to assume that where conflicts occur they are simply class based. Although the stereotypical picture of the outsider is of a middle class busybody, many incomers are people who have some links anyway. Some are the children of people who farmed in adjoining districts, farmers who have retired and sold their farms, week-enders who have been coming to an area for many years and settle permanently upon retirement. Furthermore, those people who are regarded as 'local' are not an unchanging and homogenous group anyway, they may change as new jobs, marriages and deaths impact upon their lives. As Phillips suggests, 'many of those considered to be local will be in the middle or upper classes' (1998, p39), and in some instances it is not so much the replacement of the working class by middle class incomers, as the replace-ment of a more established rural middle class by other middle class incomers. Nonetheless, one of the difficulties facing incomers to rural areas is that they are often unaware of the sorts of physical and social geographies mentioned in the previous section, and even when they are aware of them they may have difficulty establishing what these parameters and expectations are. In fact, incomers may often bring with them their *imagined geographies*, that is, their expectations about the lifestyle and the relationships that they will have in their new area:

> *Well, I think when you don't come from here you kind of think that it is a really wonderful place, it is kind of all the positive things you think about . . . you don't ever tend to think of it as being about 'backbiting' or whatever, you have this clichéd image of it being a smiling, happy place, without any hassles . . . well that's how I saw it before I came here and that's before I saw it as 'warts and all'.*
>
> (Burnett, 1996, p19)

The potential for conflict is obvious, and is evident in the following comments:

> *More English coming in. They don't belong here. They would be all right if they were part of the community, spoke Welsh. But they live as if they were still in England.*
>
> (Cloke et al., 1997, p149)

Here the clash of expectations is sharply focused around national identities and language, and it is the lack of cultural competence, in this case with language, that is seen as the main issue. Contradictory expectations can result in much wider conflicts about the influence of incomers upon the local community:

> *Welsh and English in schools is a very big issue . . . Three families wanted their children to be taught through English and it was a Welsh-medium school. It caused a big stink and a lot of upset.*
>
> (Cloke et al., 1997, p28)

In Wales and Scotland, this resentment of incomers is sometimes conceptualised quite deliberately in colonial terms, and there is a conscious invocation of a history and experience of exploitation, 'Some English come here and act like colonials—talk about us as peasants' (Cloke et al., 1997, p25). Sometimes, the imagery of colonialism is taken further in the use of the term 'white settler', which has been widely used in Scotland to derogate incomers, or at least some of them:

> *There's a lot of people who are incomers by definition but white settlers seem something apart. I think . . . a white settler would usually denote somebody*

English for a start, and kind of remained detached ... was in the community but sort of took what they wanted of it and kind of put nothing back in ... just remained in their own wee bubble ... I don't really know how to say it but it seems to me it's a very negative thing though ... a white settler.

(Burnett, 1996, p22)

Issues of cultural competence can extend to many other aspects of rural life:

... they don't know how to behave. They drive the wrong cars, put up the wrong curtains, and create pretty front gardens that just don't fit in. In the village they don't know how to greet people, how to have a real conversation. Some of them want nothing to do with us, and others would like to be part of the community, but only if they can be in charge of what goes on. They just don't know how to belong, even when they try very hard to fit in.

(Cloke et al., 1997, p150)

Although these quotations refer to local perceptions of English incomers into rural mid-Wales and Scotland, similar difficulties can arise even when the cultural distance between the parties is less marked. All these negative comments about incomers might suggest that they are universally disliked, but as ever, there is a variety of responses. Some country people make a distinction by particularising individuals, that is, distinguishing them from the broader group (Pugh, 1998). 'English people ... affect the culture ... come in with money. In principle, I don't want them here, but as human beings I treat them individually' (Cloke et al., 1997, p25). Other locals appreciate the boost to local trade and the population, 'I'm pleased to see some people living here instead of empty houses' and 'they bring money with them and pay taxes' (Cloke et al., 1997, p26). Clearly, while the reception given to incomers is a matter of individual perception, as noted in the discussion on community, the sense of identity and economic security felt by local people are important factors. In areas where there are difficulties recruiting teachers or other public servants, incomers may be welcomed for the role that they fulfil in local life. This welcome may also extend to those incomers who bring children with them and so help maintain struggling school rolls. The acceptance of incomers is also influenced by the degree of contact that other people have with them, so that, a new nurse will have more opportunities not only to meet with and be met by other people, but will have more chances for their outsider status to be overcome by an appreciation of their personal qualities. Social class and occupation are important factors too, and Burnett (1996) has noted how women's acceptance as incomers may become governed by a given status, perhaps determined partly by the occupation and social status of their husbands. The length of time that a person is settled within a community is obviously an important factor, but time alone does not usually bring with it acceptance, which mostly develops through interaction of some sort. Incoming families with children may have many opportunities to interact through their children's schooling, transport, and leisure activities.

The process of changing perceptions and acceptance of an incomer as belonging to a community is not solely a process which insiders apply to incomers, it is also a process that takes place in the mind of the incomer, as their self-identification changes. Burnett describes this as a *negotiated process of belonging*, which means that acceptance and belonging are not simply negotiated through external interactions with other people, they are also actively constructed internally in a person's self-consciousness.

> *I just call myself local now. I don't feel like an incomer any more. I did at first, but not any more . . . now I feel part of the community here.*
> (Burnett, 1996, p26)

This is a crucial point because it emphasises the importance of the subjective experience, rather than simply suggesting that a feeling of belonging is an purely objective status.

Most incomers are aware of their status and probably realise that if they wish to be accepted they have some work to do. Burnett suggests that women are more conscious of the need to develop a deep knowledge of the community and will usually work hard to acquire this. For such people, 'local knowledge is a crucial resource for it allows the incomer to comment and contradict present events in relation to past ones' (Burnett, 1996, p27). However, it is also the case that incomers who 'submerge' their own personality in an attempt to fit in, may find that this is not an effective way of operating. Such tentativeness may be perceived by other people as being overly guarded or judging behaviour and be counterproductive, and such self-denial can be erosive of any internal sense of self-worth and confidence. A personal sense of self-belonging, separate from whatever objective level of acceptance exists, is an important resource which contributes to resilience and contentment. The tensions involved in being too passive are evident in this woman's words:

> *When I first came here I was really careful, you know . . . I never got involved, never made any criticism of things. I suppose I felt it wasn't really my place. Now I just say what I like, when I like. I mean, I came to the conclusion that it was my life and it was passing me by without my involvement in it. I just thought I have as much right to say how I feel about things as the next person.*
> (Burnett, 1996, p26)

This reassertion of self is sometimes prompted by the realisation that belongingness is never a permanent and completely established process for incomers, nor for long term residents either. The idealisation of rural life, particularly the belief in a more settled and secure sense of community, can obscure this social fact. One woman who had grasped the contingent nature of acceptance, said, 'one minute I am local, and when it suits them, I am not, . . . (then) my opinions don't count' (Burnett, 1996, p26). As we shall see later in the discussion on racism, if social identity is a more fluid and conditional status than might be expected and if the work of establishing and maintaining oneself is never finished, then while this remains a continuing endeavour for everyone in a community, it has a particular significance for those whose identity may be linked to some broader and potentially 'risky' dimension of social difference, like their ethnicity, skin colour, or homosexuality.

The role of gossip

The traditional view of gossip as a negative and damaging aspect of social life is well known, and there is no doubt how powerfully it can operate to induce conformity. As the words of Elaine, an incomer to a small village, demonstrate:

> *You have to work hard to prove yourself to feel you belong. There is a lot of pressure, whereas in the city . . . you don't have to make such an effort. You have to conform to their expectations or they will . . . gossip about you.*
>
> (Hughes, 1997, p131)

> *It's hard . . . when everyone knows your business and is watching you all the time . . . a lot of people who think they have the right to judge what you do and discuss it endlessly.*
>
> (Cloke et al., 1997, p160)

Obviously, the networks of gossip as well as their content constitute an important element in the knowledge that circulates within communities, but social workers should not see it simply as a trivial or mean-spirited activity because it performs some vital functions in the social life of rural communities. Perhaps the most important is its role in the avoidance and resolution of conflict. In small, stable communities where effective working relationships with other people may have to be sustained over many years, it is not always possible nor desirable to confront issues 'head on'. The geographical distance between people and the lower levels of social contact may mean that there are fewer occasions when issues can be raised directly with another person, or for misunderstandings to be corrected. The indirect transmission of one's opinions or concerns via other people may be a more effective way of communicating in situations of potential conflict without the risks of direct contradiction or loss of face. Furthermore, apart from its cathartic effects in terms of the opportunity to ventilate one's frustrations, the act of telling a third party provides a way of testing one's views and offers the other person the opportunity to 'shape' the dialogue. Unlike social settings where there may be many observers and many participants who can intervene to prevent or avoid tensions, rural life offers fewer opportunities for such helpful interventions by third parties. Gossip in rural communities, like gossip in any community, offers the opportunity for people to say something and see if it has any effect on the behaviour of others without necessarily having to 'own' it. Thus, it may subtly shift people's attitudes and actions without either party having to directly acknowledge their position to each other. When gossip goes wrong and is perceived as having damaging consequences, it is often the result of the third party, insufficiently muting the message to make it more palatable to the recipient. Nonetheless, not all gossip is intentionally transmitted towards a specific target. In many instances, gossip is a way of establishing information about oneself or other people, and while gossip may not actually be as all-pervasive as people assume, the belief that:

> . . . *everyone knows everything about everyone else . . . is the working premise by which much rural life is conducted . . . while this cannot be accurate, the popular perception or social representation of this being so remains incredibly powerful and consequently people act upon it.*

> (Burnett, 1998, p27)

Consequently, social workers in rural areas often find that clients wish to 'place' them, that is to establish who they are and where they come from. Unlike a city, where a client would have little expectation of knowing the worker personally, or even of knowing someone else who knows the worker, in a rural area there is a good chance that they will have some knowledge of each other, or have some mutual links through other people. The exploration of these links serves several purposes. First, it can be 'safe ground' that helps to establish the working relationship. Second, it allows them to establish themselves as part of a wider community, and in particular, allows the client to show that whatever problem they are currently having to deal with, that they are in all other respects a competent and functioning member of the community. The prospective client may also test the credibility of the worker by seeing how they respond to gossip about other people, and so form some view about the likely boundaries of any confidential information that may be shared. This aspect of rural practice is discussed further in Part 3.

Gender

Much of the research upon gender in rural life has focused upon the experience of women in farming (Little, 1987, 1997; Whatmore, 1990). This work has examined the gendered divisions in work and home life, and like feminist research in other areas, has pointed up the stereotypical representations of women, the inequities in their lives, and shown how their contribution has been undervalued and under-recognised (Whatmore, 1998). The stereotypical expectations of women as mothers and homemakers in society generally, have been especially powerful in the countryside because they form part of a broader set of ideas about home life in rural communities. A quote from Rebecca, a farmer's wife in her fifties, sums up this traditional lifestyle:

> *When I was younger all the farmer's wives around me were at home; they cleaned and that is all they did. They may have gone to market one day a week ... otherwise they were at home all the week doing the cleaning and the cooking.*

(Hughes, 1997, p128)

Ideas about the traditional stability of rural life and about the rural idyll become tied into ideas about the naturalness of women's roles at home, and in the wider rural community, and have formed perhaps the most dominant discourse about their lives in the countryside (Davidoff, et al., 1976). Furthermore, the social constraints upon women, and indeed upon anyone who does not wish to conform to the gendered expectations of their roles, are more immediate, as 'deviant' behaviour is more apparent in small communities where there are few opportunities for relative anonymity. It would, however, be simplistic just to present this as something 'done' to women, like many forms of social life and social control, those whose lives are constrained by the social norms often accept, to some degree, the 'rightness' of such limiting expectations. The words of Phyllis, a mother of six children and married to a now-retired farmer epitomise this:

> *I think a woman's place was traditionally in the home and I am old-fashioned probably but I still think so ... that is what has gone wrong with society. Women going out to work and they are not doing their job at home looking after the children and the home.*

(Hughes, 1997, p130)

Interestingly, Hughes (1997), in her research into women's lives in two small villages along the English/Welsh border found that regardless of their age or whether they were incomers or locals, a 'general attitude prevailing that it was a woman's duty to stay at home with her children, particularly when ... (they) were younger' (1997, p130). Some women have no difficulty in accepting and enjoying this role, but for others the restrictive and suffocating effects of such limiting expectations reflect the negative experiences that are extensively documented in women's lives more generally. What is not always recognised is the extent to which the social and geographical situation of rural women can reinforce these constraints. Limited opportunities for paid work outside the home, lack of access to transport, and limited alternative arrangements for child care, may all contribute to social isolation and economic dependency:

> *Groups of women, such as carers, those without access to child care or transport, are effectively trapped within the home or local area and thus are denied the chance of paid employment outside of the home or locality. Although such people may not be registered as unemployed and may not be actively seeking work, since they may have come to accept their restrictive circumstances, they nevertheless represent a group which is experiencing considerable employment disadvantage.*

(Cloke et al., 1994, cited in Chapman, 1996, p8)

The continuing perception of women as a reserve labour force is evident in a report for the Rural Development Commission, which pointed out that with an ageing population and a decline in the numbers of young people starting work, rural employers would need to recruit more women. It estimated that by 2001 women will comprise 45 per cent of the formal work force in rural areas and that access to suitable child care was the most common barrier to returning to paid work (Stone, 1990). But, in the British countryside, as in the rest of Europe, child care services are generally either in short supply or do not match carers' needs very well (Cohen, 1995; Vaughan, 1996). In most rural areas the level of child care services is markedly lower than in most urban areas. Paradoxically, the opportunities for children to play in the countryside seem to be diminishing as much rough and marginal land has been brought into production (National Children's Play and Recreation Unit, 1992), and as adult tolerance of children roaming around seems to have diminished.

The role of women in creating and sustaining the social networks of the countryside is a significant one. Little (1997), in her research found that 'Women were seen, and saw themselves, for example, as in many ways responsible for the protection, preservation and continuation of the village community' (1997, p153). In short, 'Women hold the village together' (Little, 1997, p153), by undertaking the organisation of local events, by 'keeping an eye' on those residents who were elderly and infirm, or had been ill, or otherwise struggling to cope in some way. The Women's Institute is generally one of the most significant formal organisations, though activities centred around a local church or chapel often provide a focus for the 'social' work that women do in rural communities. Wenger provides a typical example of such care:

(Mrs Griffiths) . . . continued to be a faithful member of the chapel and a good friend to the schoolteacher for whom she had cleaned. The schoolteacher was now suffering from the early stages of dementia and Mrs Griffiths visited her regularly and monitored and valeted her personal appearance. If she knew anyone was ill or recently bereaved, Mrs Griffiths could be relied on to visit and offer support and help.

(Wenger, 1994, p70)

These 'care-giving' and socially productive forms of activity are important aspects of the way many rural women view themselves, and may have implications for their sense of self worth and for their health needs in older age. An American study of older women's health preferences found that although the absence of illness was, as one might expect, a dominant theme in their responses, there was also the importance they placed upon seeing themselves as self-reliant people who were able to help and support others. However, they did not always have corresponding expectations that others would or should provide for them, though most felt that they had friends whom they could talk to and that some family members would support them. Significantly, most respondents did not generally associate health with any sense of satisfaction in their daily lives, even though they did acknowledge the negative effects of stress (DePoy and Butler, 1996). Clearly, low expectations in terms of one's own health and life satisfaction are potentially risky features, and DePoy and Butler suggest that:

. . . promoting the health of rural women may involve considering how to maintain their role as caregivers without imposing it . . . (and that) . . . they would benefit from educational and support services to help them develop expectations for life satisfaction and engage proactively in meeting their own needs.

(DePoy and Butler, 1996, p219)

Wenger (1994), has pointed out that older women in the countryside are more likely to be widowed than men, because they marry men older than themselves, and men die younger, and because proportionately fewer of their generation married anyway, are more likely to be living alone, and also to be living alone for longer periods compared to men in similar situations. In her study in North Wales, she found that 'more than half the women . . .

lived alone compared with less than a quarter of the men' (1994, p62), and also, that older women are more likely to report that they rely on themselves, or on a member of another household, rather than on men. Furthermore, because different women adopted different patterns of adaptation to old age, those who were more self-contained in their social networks were less likely to ask for or accept help from others. Nevertheless, it is clear that regardless of individual patterns of adaptation that:

> *... as a result of differential longevity, women who survive into old age are more likely to be living alone and as a result are likely to adopt far more self-sufficient and independent lifestyles than old men. The drive to retain autonomy and independence in old age is a dominant theme ...*
>
> (Wenger, 1994, p83)

While individual women's lives in the countryside may vary considerably, many of the features of their lives more generally mirror those of urban women's lives, in changing patterns of family life, the experience of separation and divorce, increased participation in formal employment, the juggling of multiple roles, poor pay, and restricted career opportunities (Gieve, 1989). We should not assume that the ways in which women are seen, as well as the ways in which they view themselves and live their lives, are homogenous or universal. There may be considerable variation arising from individual personality and preference, as well as from other structural factors like age, social class, and ethnicity. Nevertheless, the point, as Little emphasises, is that there are 'a set of powerful assumptions . . . about gender identities in rural communities . . . which influences the behaviour, values and expectations of all rural women and men' (1997, p155). Of course, some of these expectations may be found in urban areas, but it seems that they may be more dominant in rural communities.

Changing roles?

Women currently comprise just over a quarter of the regularly employed agricultural work force (Annual Abstract of Statistics, 1999), and are an increasingly large proportion of the seasonal and casual work force in the UK. In fact, across Europe, women are 'increasingly being integrated into Europe's waged farm work force. They make up 54 per cent of part-time and 40 per cent of the seasonal or casual farm work force' (Whatmore, 1998, p5). Chapman and her colleagues, in a six year study of low income and employment in rural Britain (1998), found that there was a significant growth in the number of hours worked by women, and that rural women's wages have grown more rapidly than those of women in urban areas, and somewhat surprisingly, that their wages were growing faster than those of rural men. The relative differences in growth probably reflects the lower base levels of women's wages relative to men's in the first place, and it remains the case that women's jobs are often insecure and low paid, and their prospects are often hampered by the lack of career opportunities for them in rural areas (Stren and Turbin, 1986).

As noted earlier, some commentators on country life tend to ignore the roles that women play, and often render them invisible in their androcentric (male-focused) analyses of rural matters. However, to look at women's roles in isolation from men's can lead to a narrow perspective upon gender identities in rural life (Hughes, 1997), and can result in a rather deterministic portrayal, in which women are inevitably disadvantaged. The realities of women's lives are somewhat more complex. For example, because many small farms are dependent upon both partners in a relationship working on the farm, many women develop a considerable range of skills that are not traditionally seen as 'feminine' ones. Although women make a substantial contribution which neither they nor their partners always recognise (Gieve, 1989), many women, through handling machinery, livestock, contractors and suppliers, as well as the accounts, do have a secure sense of their own worth and their capabilities. A worth that is often explicitly and implicitly recognised by their partners, albeit alongside other rather traditional notions. As one Welsh farmer, put it:

I don't know where I'd be without her really, she can turn her hand to anything on the farm. She'll do what's needed, when it's needed and still gets dinner on the table at night.

(quoted in Ashton, 1994, p128)

A craft worker, quoted by Fisher, epitomises a more self-aware sense of crossing the boundaries of traditional gender roles when she said, 'I bought my first saw with my Maternity Benefit' (1997, p232). In such circumstances, these supposedly 'non-traditional' divisions of labour has implications for the extent and styles of involvement in decision making adopted by farming couples (Berlan, 1988). In addition, as Whatmore has suggested:

. . . there is some evidence that patriarchal gender relations in family farming are increasingly being contested. Younger European rural women are leaving the land, unwilling to accept the conventional status of a farmer's wife and the limited opportunities for entering farming as a successor or business principal in their own right . . . As women who enter farming through marriage are increasingly drawn from non-farming backgrounds, traditional practices and values are coming under renewed pressure for change.

(Whatmore, 1998, p5)

37

However, as Westwood and Bhachu noted, 'Women working with their husbands in small businesses, where they don't receive a wage, are in a position which reproduces dependency very similar to that of domestic labour' (1988, p6). Nevertheless, ever since the Arts and Crafts movement of the 1890s and early 1900s, some men and women have consciously sought to work in the countryside as an escape from the mechanisation of industrial society. The home-based production of craft work in wood, ceramics and textiles, continues to be seen as a personally liberating choice. For example, Sam, a woman marquetry maker, said:

> We've done things because we don't like the mainstream. People have not dropped out, but said, 'Look, I don't want to be involved in going in to a job nine to five, clocking in and clocking out, getting money and that's your life ... you're not in control of what goes on. People want to be in control of their own lives.
>
> (Fisher, 1997, p240)

It is also evident that the liberating aspect of such home-based work has been deliberately sought by women who are very clear about what their choices represent. For example, Rhian, a silversmith, said that such crafts allowed women 'to express maybe a different sexuality, or work ethos or mentality' (Fisher, 1997, p240). Of course, one should be wary of over-romanticising home-based production, especially since it fits so easily with the more general 'idyllisation' of rural life, for as we shall see in the sections on 'domestic violence' and social isolation, there are some real problems too. The complexity and variability of the experiences of rural women also arise from the fact that women do not exist simply as rural or urban women, but as members of particular age groups, social classes, ethnic groups, and so on (Whatmore, 1998). It is therefore vital that workers do not unwittingly reproduce gendered expectations of women, and men, and do not overlook important information about women and their particular situations.

Social Problems, Discrimination and Disadvantage

Social problems in the countryside are often unrecognised, and this invisibility stems from two factors. First, the relatively less dense patterns of settlement, especially outside of the villages, means that problems of poverty, loneliness and so on, may be less visible to the wider society. Even when problems are recognised, it can be difficult, because of the relative geographical isolation for individuals and agencies, to respond effectively and this issue is developed further in Parts 2 and 3. Second, the tendency to idealise rural life, which, as we see in the following sub-section on racism contributes to the formation of the problem, can also make it less likely that people will perceive even the existence of a problem at all. Without recognition there can be no action and no response. This section reviews three main problems which have been the subject of reliable studies, namely rural isolation, racism, and poverty. However, there are other issues such as 'domestic violence', drug misuse, and homophobia, where there is relatively little research on the particularities of these problems in rural areas, as opposed to urban ones, and further reference will be made to these problems later in the book. In each of the following three problems discussed, there are factors that distinguish the way in which the problems emerge, are experienced, and are sometimes exacerbated by the rural context, and throughout, I have tried to show some of the general effects of say, poverty or racism, without suggesting that they have inevitable and unvarying consequences.

In many instances, rural dwellers may hold derogatory and damaging stereotypical ideas about particular groups and yet, at a personal level, operate with courtesy and respect towards individual members of such devalued categories. Although a further discussion of how such processes of generalisation and particularisation operate is beyond the scope of this book, it is worth noting in the following excerpts how often the process of particularisation, when an individual is treated as an 'exception', liberates them from the otherwise discriminatory effects of stereotypes (Pugh, 1998). The recognition that such 'freeing up' of expectations is not a permanent, but a conditional acceptance, does not detract from the fact that it can create the space in which a given individual can make their life somewhat different, and more positive, than we might otherwise expect.

Rural isolation

In the earlier sections, I noted the importance of understanding how a sense of belonging is developed and how important it can be in personal identity. Feelings of isolation are not linked solely to the objective facts about the amount, distance and degree of contact with other people, though these obviously are important factors, but are experienced subjectively. The degree to which a person feels isolated is strongly influenced by a range of subjective factors, including:

- Whether a person perceives themselves as belonging to a particular community or place.
- Whether a person operates mentally within a wider social landscape.
- The extent to which an individual feels that they are in control of their life.
- Personal expectations about what their life should be like.
- Experiences of change and loss.

Demographic changes may also have an impact upon the degree of social interaction that people have, and in some areas depopulation is a factor, while smaller families form a more general trend that reduces the number of people who are potentially available to provide social contact and support. A study in rural North Wales found that older women who lived alone spent much more time on their own than older men in the same situation:

Nearly twice as many women, 38 per cent, as men, 20 per cent, spent nine or more hours a day alone and for most this meant they were alone all day and all night . . . it is not surprising then to find that women are more likely to feel lonely.

(Wenger, 1994, p62)

In contrast, because of the patterns of marriage and mortality, with women tending to marry men older than themselves, and men dying earlier than women, older men are more likely to still be living with their partner, and also to have sisters who may provide care for them if they have no surviving wife or daughter. But we should not assume that loneliness and isolation are inevitable or even typical of older women's experiences. As Wenger states, 'an understanding of support networks is crucial to an understanding of the experience of ageing and to the nature of identity in old age' (1994, p62). From her research, she has identified three factors which influence the type and extent of network formation for older women:

- Chance—for 'much depends upon the marriages and fertility of earlier generations, the size of one's family, of socialisation and even birth order' (1994, p62).
- Migration—the influence of geographical relocation and the time in life at which it occurs.
- Personality and temperament—'those who are loners in old age tend to be those who have been loners all their lives'.

(1994, p63)

But, while some variations of personality traits may decrease the likelihood of forming and maintaining social contacts, 'even the most gregarious temperament cannot alter the effects of biology and migration. It can only affect adaptation to the outcomes of these factors' (1994, p63).

Rural isolation is potentially problematic for anyone whose capacity to engage with others is impaired or limited in some way, whether this be caused by physical, social, mental or material factors. The problems of mothers with young children were noted earlier, but while many studies point out the lack of child care facilities, few devote much attention to the issue of mothers' social isolation. The question of these women's needs is almost always subsumed by consideration of their role as mothers, so potential links to other problems like isolation and mental health are not explored. Poverty and disability can often result in limited contact with wider social networks, especially when access to telephones and transport is barred by cost and availability.

The isolation for people with mental health problems in rural areas is often reinforced by the lack of understanding and sometimes outright hostility shown towards them (Pugh and Richards, 1996). Social isolation by virtue of difference is also experienced by other groups and individuals. For example, there are few informal networks for gay men and women in rural areas, and this often compounds the difficulties experienced by some men and women in establishing for themselves their sexual identity, for there are few places where it is possible to meet and talk with others and to try out different identities and experience different degrees of 'coming out'. Of course, none of these factors operate apart from other aspects of a person's social location, so the effects of being socially different or marginalised are not always predictable. As Roni Crwydren's experience shows so clearly:

I was born, and have spent most of my life, in one small area about which I feel deeply and passionately. I feel comfortable and at home in its woods, on its hills, moors and cliffs. Coming from an 'alternative' background . . . and from a family of English-speaking outsiders in what was still a very Welsh area, I have not, in the past, been accustomed to feeling at home amongst Welsh people to the same extent. Being an outsider was, therefore, such a natural part of me, that choosing to become a lesbian did not mean risking rejection from society, friends, colleagues and acquaintances, or leaving my home area, as it does for so many lesbians.

(Crwydren, 1994, p294)

This account shows how a sense of belonging to a place and already having some outsider status provides a basis upon which other aspects of identity can be built. However, as we shall see in the discussion of racism, we should not assume that any identity is a permanent accomplishment, it is always an active process and this brings with it the possibility of change for better or worse. For rural dwellers from ethnic minorities, this may also be complicated by a situation of double isolation, where they do not 'fit in' with the local community and are also physically distanced from other members of their ethnic communities.

Racism

Over the last few years there has been an increasing recognition that racism is a problem in rural areas (Ageyman, 1989; Dhalech, 1999; Jay, 1992; Nizhar,

1995; Sibley, 1995), but many people still find it difficult to accept this. It is likely that their reluctance to accept the existence of racism in rural areas follows from a lack of knowledge and from a misunderstanding of what racism is. Many people are unaware of the extent of ethnic and 'racial' differentiation in rural areas and they simply assume that there are very few people from ethnic minorities in the countryside. However, while it is true that the majority of Britain's ethnic minority population live in the metropolitan and urban areas, as the earlier section on population statistics showed, there are settled minority groups in every county of England and Wales, and in most counties in Scotland (Office of National Statistics, 1997). It is also the case that many people still misunderstand the nature of racism and often persist in seeing it as a 'numbers' problem (Cashmore and Troyna, 1983). That is, they see the roots of racism arising from the presence of ethnic diversity. Therefore, if racism is perceived as a response to the actual presence of black people, then there can be no racism in the countryside because, in their minds, black people are largely absent from rural Britain. This mistaken view fails to recognise how racism is a form of discrimination in Britain which is predominantly constructed and enacted by the 'white' majority, and is also somewhat self-serving because it conveniently absolves those who hold it from any responsibility to act, by locating the causes of racism with other people.

In the introduction to this chapter, the point was made that ideas about the countryside often carry powerful symbolic information about who the countryside is for, and about ideas of identity and otherness. There is a long history of linkage between ideas of rurality and notions of ethnic purity, and from the nineteenth century onwards:

> *The countryside, at the core of Britain's national identity, was regarded as the ideal location in which to breed a healthy and moral 'race'* . . . *(often)* . . . *The purity of rural areas was juxtaposed with the pollution of urban industry and commerce, and cities were aligned with racial degeneration.*
>
> (Ageyman and Spooner, 1997, p200)

Similar ideas have been explicitly embraced and espoused by right wing parties such as the British National Party, the National Front (Coates, 1993; Jay, 1992), and implicitly by the Conservative Party. Each of these organisa-tions, albeit in different ways, has attempted to idealise the countryside and rural life, and at the heart of their efforts is an attempt to present an homogenised history and undifferentiated conception of British culture—a unified idea of a single and 'pure' culture to which we should apparently aspire. Consequently, social differences which contradict or complicate this idealisation are minimised or 'disappeared'. This is evident in the way in which 'British' is often used as a synonym for 'English', thus collapsing the Celtic countries into a monolithic entity. While many people are familiar with the notion that history has typically been presented as 'his-story' and has written out the role of women, they may be less aware of the extent to which black people have, and continue to be, written out of the script for Britain. But, as both Ageyman (1995), and Fryer (1984), have shown, from Roman times on, there is a long history of black people in Britain whose presence and influence have been ignored. That the names Olaudah Equiano (freed slave, writer, anti-slavery campaigner and noted public figure, about 1745–1797), Mancherjee Merwanjee Bhownagree (Conservative MP for Bethnal Green 1895–1906), and Mary Seacole (healer and nursing pioneer, about 1805–1881), mean nothing to most people in Britain is evidence of this. Fryer records that, 'Though their largest concentration was in London, black people were scattered all over England in the second half of the century (the seventeenth). Parish records ... show a black presence in Plymouth, Bedfordshire, Essex and Cumberland' (1984, p32). Furthermore, newspaper reports and other records show that black slaves were to be found in many other rural districts in England and Wales at this time. The point is that the omission or ignorance of the actual presence of black people, both historically and contemporaneously, not only fosters the myth of 'purity' for some people, it allows others to disregard the realities of racism in rural areas.

In many ways, the manifestations of racism in rural areas are the same as in urban areas. Those who are perceived as different, and especially those who are perceived as black may be marginalised, they have greater difficulty in securing jobs that are commensurate with their experience and qualifications, and are more likely to be abused and attacked than other people (Myers, 1995). Dhalech (1999), reports examples of the cases that came to the attention of the Rural Race Equality project in Devon, Cornwall and Somerset, and the following extracts are typical of incidents that occur throughout the countryside:

The client is female, 36 years old, Black Caribbean, married. Husband is employed on farm as a maintenance engineer and they have no alternative but to live in a small village in tied accommodation. Client's son, 11 years old, was approached by an adult male at the end of the boy's drive. The boy was walking his two dogs, both on leads and under control ... The man kicked the dog who leapt and bit the man as it was protecting its owner. Man threatened boy verbally with the police and having his dog put down. Client's family keep a low profile in the village as they believe they are not viewed as 'normal' residents.

(Dhalech, 1999, p2)

Client . . . has had a brick through her window, human excrement on her doorstep and lighted cigarettes through the letterbox. Client moved from Leicester to take up her first job. She had never suffered any racial abuse in Leicester and was surprised at finding racism in a rural area.

(Dhalech, 1999, p24)

Racism in rural areas, is, of course not confined to the public at large. Dhalech reports two other examples which arise from public officials:

At 1.30 a.m. my son and I walked from my house . . . A police van with a dog passed us . . . 50 yards away from my house we were confronted by two plain clothes policemen and the police van driver who immediately got his dog out. My son asked officers for their numbers. They refused. My son was threatened with the dog being set loose on him, I was searched. I told them I was a social worker who was getting air with his son, we were then told we could go. The police told us that a neighbour had reported two suspicious characters lurking about; I believe this to be untrue.

(Dhalech, 1999, p4)

Woman (Indian) resident in the UK 20 years or more applied to go on a course at the local college. Interviewed, but turned down on the basis that she 'would not mix in' with other students.

(Dhalech, 1999, p10)

Even when racism does not seem to be overt, the presence of black people in the countryside runs counter to many people's expectations, as Myers states 'For everyday white country folk it appears that blacks undermine the concept of bucolic bliss' (1995, p5). The stereotyping and stigmatisation of blackness is implicit therefore, in the conception of the countryside as 'white' and of black people as 'trouble'.

However, we should be wary of assuming that the lives of all ethnic minorities in the countryside are constantly blighted by racism. Iris Braithwaite, who was born in Barbados, described her experience in an otherwise all-white community in the Northamptonshire countryside , thus:

We had good neighbours . . . Nothing was too difficult for them. And that made it simpler for us to settle in. We never had any bad neighbours. Most people around here were the same age as us. We were all thinking about earning a living, getting children into school and getting on . . . people would come over for a couple of drinks or suggest a picnic or a walk through the forest.

(Myers, 1995, p5)

Another young black man from the same area said:

Having grown up with the countryside so close, the thing is I don't like cities. They're full of hustle and bustle and people with unpleasant manners. Around here I can cycle into town through the fields.

(Myers, 1995, p5)

For many people who live there, their experience in a small community is one in which they can be accepted on their own merits and are able to establish their own identity away from some of the stifling expectations of other larger communities. Being black, or, as we shall see later, different in other ways, can be a peculiarly exposed experience in the countryside, though not inevitably a negative one. However, although the experience of country life may be a liberating one, we should not forget that the potential threat of racism is always present and cannot be avoided in some of the ways that are possible in urban areas. There is rarely immediate support available from a larger community of people with similar backgrounds and similar experiences, and there is no escape to the anonymity of a larger group. Charlotte Williams, a Welsh Guyanese woman who grew up in a small town in North Wales, captured this sense of isolation and vulnerability well, when she wrote:

I'm not Cardiff black. There's no Tiger Bay in my story. I have no rememberings of such a vibrant and supportive black community; no sense of that collective identity won through association and revisited in talk . . . At any moment some aspect of your visibility could be called forth for negative comment or more benignly negative connotation.

(Williams, 1997, pp25–6)

For many ethnic minorities, this sense in which one's identity is always potentially a point of issue, either for oneself in resisting and responding to the marginalising tendencies of the wider society, or for others who may use it in myriad ways to attack, scapegoat or otherwise discriminate, can create a condition of continuing uncertainty. A position in which ordinary things that might be taken for granted by much of Britain's white population are never settled matters for many ethnic minorities. Seemingly simple choices as to whether to eat at a particular pub, patronise a particular shop, or ask for help from public services, all become potentially risky encounters whose outcomes are uncertain, in ways that most white people would not even have to consider.

Poverty

Despite numerous reports into rural poverty and some widely publicised studies, such as that undertaken by the Anglican Church (*Faith in the*

45

Countryside), poverty is still perceived by many people to be an urban phenomenon. As Furuseth has noted, even:

Recent debates over welfare reform and discussions over an underclass culture make it clear that the public and elected officials seem fixated on poverty as an urban issue.

(1998, p233)

Unfortunately, poverty is a persistent feature of rural life and, as in urban areas, contributes greatly to the broader levels of deprivation experienced by some people and groups in the countryside. There are two distinctive features of poverty in rural areas which differ from poverty in urban areas. The first is that in many villages and small communities the poor often live quite close to those who are comparatively rich. This can be a source of friction as either group may be less tolerant of the others' way of living. For example, the wealthier inhabitants of communities may dislike the presence of old broken down vehicles which the poor see as a potential resource, as a source of spare parts or maybe to be 'fixed up' one day. In contrast, the poor may resent the power and influence that the wealthier residents wield within the community, by virtue of their wealth and their participation in the governance of the community. This close contact is also a source of information, and so the poor may become much more aware of their comparative disadvantage, while the wealthy may realise that poverty and unemployment is not necessarily a consequence of personal inadequacy. In fact, they may, in some circumstances, be more sympathetic to improved social provision and action. The second distinctive feature of poverty in the countryside is that it may not be as visible because of the lower population density and the relative privacy or isolation of many people. In fact, even when the signs of rural poverty are obvious, as in the run-down condition of an old cottage, it is often perceived benignly or romanticised as part of the bucolic image of rural life, in a way that would be unimaginable for its equivalent in the city (Furuseth, 1998). Consequently, there is a tendency to see poverty solely as an urban problem, and certainly, in a comparative sense, poverty is less widespread. Research in twelve areas of rural England by Cloke et al. (1994), found that the proportion of those who were 'in or on the margins of poverty' was generally over 20 per cent, and in the worst area, over 39 per cent.

A small study within Wiltshire found that '40 per cent of adult workers were earning gross salaries of less than £8,000 and 11.5 per cent of the population were in receipt of housing benefit or council tax rebate' (SSI, 1998b, p7). A much larger study into employment and low incomes, funded by the Joseph Rowntree Foundation concluded that:

Proportionately fewer individuals receive lower incomes in rural areas, spells of low income tend to be shorter, and the proportion of those who are 'persistently poor' is less. Nevertheless, one in three individuals in rural areas experienced low income during the five years, 1991–96 (the duration of the study).

(Joseph Rowntree Foundation, 1998, p1)

So, while the incidence of poverty in rural areas appears to be less than in urban districts, it is clear that it is still a relatively common problem, and as most social workers who work in rural areas realise, low income is a very significant factor in determining the life chances and quality of life of many of the people with whom they work. The low levels of income may arise through low wages generally, from seasonally fluctuating employment, or from having to live on social security benefits. Low pay is common in the countryside, and, as in the rest of the UK, there are marked gender differences in wages. For example, in 1998 the average weekly earnings for manual workers employed in agriculture, hunting and forestry were £260.30 for men and £185.7 for women, and while men's average wages have risen by £23 since 1995, women's average earnings have only risen by £10.40 in the same period. A more broadly based comparison of men's and women's wages in these industries in 1997, including all jobs and not just manual labour, indicates a similar but less marked disparity, in that men's average weekly earnings were £261.40, while women's were £201.66, and that these levels were based on men working 46.6 hours on average, and women working 42.6 hours on average. By comparison, average earnings in manual jobs in manufacturing industries in 1998 were £352.60 per week for men, and £224.20 for women (Annual Abstract of Statistics, 1999). While these statistics which show such low average incomes do not include those who are self-employed, either on large or small farms, neither do they include the spouses or partners of farmers. Thus, they do not reveal the scale of unwaged work done by women on many small farms and their subsequent economic deprivation.

One feature of rural employment noted in the Rowntree study was reduced mobility in terms of wage levels, either up or down, as compared to urban areas, and this effect was gendered, in that the chances of improving income through finding a better paid job were markedly less for women than men. The relatively high levels of self-employment, particularly of small farmers, comprising, according to Cloke et al., 1997, up to 38 per cent in some areas, leaves many people vulnerable to poverty when work is scarce or when prices fall and income declines. The reduced access to welfare benefits for self-employed workers also compounds their difficulties.

A further difficulty for those whose accommodation is tied to their employment, is that losing their job also results in losing their home. Consequently, the effects of unemployment such as reduced income are immediately worsened by the need to find somewhere else to live.

Money, of course, is usually the most important single factor contributing to deprivation, but for a number of reasons, poverty should not be seen simply as a matter of income levels. The existence of other resources, private or public, can have a marked effect upon the impact of poverty upon a particular person or family. While, say, the capacity to grow food or to collect wood as fuel still has some bearing on how badly low income may affect living standards in rural areas, the range of private resources extends to other factors, such as the level of support available from friends and relatives, the use of a motor car, access to a telephone, and so on (Townsend, 1979). In general, public resources, such as public transport, public leisure facilities, advice centres, and so on, are less evident in most rural areas and, where they do exist, certainly more difficult to access. So the deprivation that results from low incomes in rural areas may be compounded by an inability to benefit from other community resources. This is particularly true of public services such as health, housing, and leisure. However, we should be wary of assuming that the experience of poverty in the countryside is a common experience that is universally shared. For:

> ... people living in the same place, with access to similar levels of housing, service and employment opportunities, and with similar levels of wealth and income, may experience rural life differently. Their needs may be different; their expectations may be different; their willingness to cope with problems as part of everyday life may be different; their cultural view of what rural life should be like may be different; their strategies for coping with rural life may be different, and so on. Rural problems are thus experiential as well as material, and seemingly similar material conditions obscure important differences in the way that rural people feel marginalised by a lack of power, choice and opportunity, or in the way that they cope with the strong relative differences in rural life which are accentuated as the affluent live cheek by jowl with the less affluent ...

(Cloke et al., 1997, p165)

These subjective dimensions of lived experience are crucial to understanding poverty in any context. While there have been numerous studies into rural poverty (Cloke et al., 1995; Lowe et al., 1996; Mason and Taylor, 1990; Shucksmith et al., 1995; Walker, 1978), there is a lack of research into the experience of poverty in rural areas. However, a rather dated study by Fabes et al. (1983), suggested that individual responses ranged from, 'a fatalistic

48

acceptance of a lowly position within a clearly demarcated social hierarchy; a high tolerance of poverty, with people 'scraping by' for as long as possible . . . lack of material aspirations . . . and a stigmatic burden of shame and secrecy' (Cloke, 1997, pp256–7). For example, Tom Stuart, an elderly Scotsman of 90, who had never spent more than two nights away from the house he was born in, summed up his own approach to life with these words:

I suppose I'm a dying breed . . . People won't live this way again. But I was happy. I wouldn't change a thing if I could go back and do it all again. It's fate that decides what's before you; there's no point in taking too much notice of what you can't control.

(Seenan, 1999, p6)

It is difficult to ascertain whether this uncomplaining stoicism is still a feature of rural life, as it may be more representative of the perspective of an older generation, but as Cloke has shown, some rural people still see poverty in a fairly undifferentiated way and tend towards an 'idyllised' perception of rural life in which they appear reluctant to concede that they, or any one else, is in poverty:

Deprivation? I don't know what you mean. We all help each other. (Warwickshire)

There is no deprivation—if you are used to living in the town you think differently to people living in the country and vice versa. (Wiltshire)

I suppose that those people that live in the countryside have more simple ideas and don't feel deprived. (Northumberland)

It seems that people have lower expectations in rural areas, so they put up with it. (Shropshire)

(Cloke, 1997 p261)

Certainly, the findings of a more recent study by Shucksmith and Chapman (1998), which concluded that ' . . . rural people's subjective assessment of their poverty or disadvantage was often at odds with the objective definition of low income applied' (p232), tends to support this interpretation, as' . . . most respondents felt that the benefits of living in a rural area outweighed the disadvantages . . . (they) placed a high value on the non-monetary aspects of rural life' (pp232–3). However:

. . . we must also recognise elements of what Bourdieu (1984), calls the 'choice of the necessary', an attempt to present one's way of life about which one may have few choices, as a conscious preference.

(Ching and Creed, 1997, p18)

The increasing political activism of small farmers whose incomes have dropped sharply in the past few years suggest that complacency and fatalism is not universally shared. Nevertheless, it does seem to be the case that rural people do consciously weigh up the advantages and disadvantages of their situations and many conclude that their overall situation in the countryside is preferable to living in towns and cities. For example, a study in rural Wales (Esslemont and Harrington, 1991), found that when mothers were asked about the advantages and disadvantages of bringing their children up in the countryside, the majority rated the healthy environment, safety and security, mental well-being, the learning experience and the sense of community, very highly. In contrast, the difficulties in travel, a lack of access to transport, the additional expense of travel, and a general lack of facilities in terms of shops, leisure, choice of schooling and cultural experiences, were seen as considerable disadvantages, but most thought that the advantages outweighed the disadvantages. However, as Cloke et al. (1995), have pointed out, this can lead policy makers into an interesting construction of the position of the poor in rural areas, with poverty being seen as the deprivation of the advantages of urban life rather than about low income per se. Thus, intervention on behalf of the rural poor can be avoided if they are perceived as being content with their lot, that is, their material position is obscured by assuming that the disadvantages are offset by the other benefits of rural life.

Conclusion

By now, it should be evident to the reader that there is no simple picture of life in the British countryside, and complexity and variation are as evident in rural lives as in urban ones. The idealisation or idyllisation of the countryside as it is presented in country lifestyle magazines, in children's literature, and in the media generally, presents an homogenised picture of people living relatively traditional lives in safe communities where children are free to roam and play, and supposedly remain more 'innocent' than city children. This idealisation masks the complexity of changes in gender roles, ignores the problems of poverty and the existence of other social problems like violence and drug abuse, and most significantly, contains little reference to other dimensions of social differentiation. Consequently, while women are typically presented in rather traditional roles as carers and homemakers, ethnic minorities, gypsies and travellers are almost entirely absent from the general pictures of rural life.

The misrepresentation of country life is often accompanied by misperceptions and oversimplifications of the subtleties and complexities of the changes occurring in rural society. For example, while there is no doubt that some older people have been left socially stranded by the decline of their communities and the movement of their adult children to alternative sources of employment in urban areas, they are not the only ones. The increasing polarisation of social class has also undermined the social and economic networks of the poorer sections of rural society. The decline of public transport in rural areas has left those with limited, or no access at all to private transport, literally stranded. At the same time economic and demographic changes have undermined the viability of many of those institutions of rural life around which a sense of community often revolved. The age, affluence and social class of those who now use the countryside as their 'dormitory', but work elsewhere, or have retired to live in the country, means that they are less likely to have school-age children, and when they do have them are less likely to use local schools. These changes have been extensive and interact together to irremediably alter the nature of rural life in many areas. The increasing secularisation of modern life and the decline in religious observance has had its effects too. In many areas, the diminishing numbers of chapels and churches, and the decline in rural schools, shops, post offices and pubs has eroded the very heart of the community. The deleterious effects of many of these changes have fallen disproportionately upon women and children and upon the poorer sections of rural communities who, because of lack of access to transport, lack of choice and alternative options, as well as the lack of other resources, are sometimes stranded without the old networks which sustained and supported their lives. Consequently, while the geographical isolation of rural lives has been reduced in some ways by technology, like the telephone, TV, and the Internet, in other respects it has been reinforced by the lack of access of many people to this new technology.

The tendency to oversimplify the realities of country life, whether it be through idealisation or misunderstanding and omission, is potentially very detrimental to the provision of effective social services. While the next chapter deals with the questions of how social service agencies should recognise and respond to the challenges and the diversity of needs in rural areas, there is a more immediate issue. Namely, how individual workers use the knowledge that they have about the rural context. The most pressing issue is how to acquire and develop knowledge about particular groups and particular problems without then presuming that all individuals in such situations will necessarily 'fit the pattern'. Thus:

... while being black or disabled in British society may be highly predictive of group experiences, it is not inevitably so for individual members of such groups.

While we can be reasonably accurate in predicting the general consequences of racism or disability, the particular experience of individuals is less certain. They may be protected by other factors or resources such as family life and social supports, political beliefs, religions and ideologies, wealth, class, and occupation.

(Pugh, 1997, p8)

We need to understand that a person's social position is located on many dimensions of social difference. Individuals are located differently in terms of their age, sexuality, ethnicity, gender, class, and so on. Consequently, in one situation at a given time, a person's age and gender may be the dominant features of his or her relations with others, while at another time and place, it may be ethnic origins and culture which predominate. Furthermore, while social identities may appear relatively stable, they are not fixed, but are produced and constructed by social interaction. Thus, social contexts and circumstances change, and as individuals and groups act, there is a complex interaction between different social factors and different demographic bases of identity which makes it impossible to know in advance just how a particular individual or group may be experiencing their problems. Of course, the practical implication of this understanding is the traditional imperative in social work—to 'start from where the client is'. That is, to avoid imposing our own meanings onto the subjective experience of others. But much of what is distinctive in social work practice arises from the intermediate location that we occupy between individuals, families and small groups, and the apparatus of the state. This location provides privileged access to the experience of other people, especially those who are socially marginalised, and provides direct evidence of the impact of statute and policy on their lives. Thus, we have to appreciate the subjective experience of individuals, however uncomfortable that may be, without losing sight of our own position and role. We need to be able to make links between their individual subjectivities and the wider context which shapes and constrains their lives, but does not completely control them (Pugh and Thompson, 1999).

Seen in this way, the rural context in which social work is undertaken is a fascinating place. How else can we understand how the idealisation of the 'rural' impacts upon our perceptions of social problems, upon our ideas of who 'belongs' in the countryside, and upon whose needs are recognised? The countryside, far from being a separate dimension of social life, can be understood as playing an important role for the whole of society. Conflicts about such things as land use, farming, travellers, hunting, and so on, may directly reflect wider conflicts about the nature of British society. For example, what is often not recognised is the way in which 'rural issues' are part of a continuing process of 'class formation', especially of the English middle classes:

The rural domain is reassuring to the middle class. It is a place where gender and ethnic identities can be anchored in 'traditional' ways, far (but not far enough?), from the fragmented, 'mixed-up' city. Within the rural domain identities are fixed, making it a white, English, family-oriented, middle-class space; a space moreover, that is imbued with its own mythical history, which selects and deploys particular, natavistic (sic) notions of what it is to belong to the national culture. That this is what attracts middle-class in-migrants to the countryside is rarely made explicit. Instead, the rural is extolled for the virtues of peace and quiet, of community and neighbourliness . . . the assertion of this form of rurality necessitates the exclusion of other social groups, usually under the guise of excluding development . . . such groups are increasingly unwelcome in the reconstituted spaces of southern England. (Thus) concern for the rural environment can be translated into the desire to protect a particular social space for the benefit of a privileged social group. Fighting to maintain the rural environment and struggling against development, is a more acceptable endeavour than seeking to exclude the less well off.

(Murdoch and Marsden, 1994, p232)

The aim of this chapter was to establish the rural context in which social work services have to operate and in particular, to demonstrate that rural life is not simple, but is shaped by complex interactions between different economic, social and geographic factors. The point is that there is not one rural life, but many. The rural context spans from the lived experience of remote hill farming families in Wales, Scotland and the north of England, through to the more prosperous and comfortable existence of the English lowlands, but whatever the specifics of particular lives, as we shall see in the next chapter, good practice can only be built upon good knowledge.

Part 2: Planning and Developing Services

It is obvious from Part 1 that the provision of personal social services in rural areas poses particular difficulties for statutory and independent organisations. Many of these difficulties arise from distance, poor transport, and sparse populations, which offer few possibilities for economies of scale and result in relatively high per capita service costs. These difficulties are in turn exacerbated for some would-be service users, by the lack of other financial or social resources which they could mobilise to meet their needs. Poverty, sexism, and racism, along with other types of discrimination, can lead to disadvantages which are not unique to the countryside, but are reinforced by the rural context. The aim of Part 2 is to point up the importance of the processes of policy development and service planning, and to show some of the ways in which these can be enhanced to provide more appropriate and responsive services. It also contains some general material that is relevant to the development of services in urban areas, but it is included because its omission would otherwise result in a rather patchy discussion if these aspects were developed solely from a rural perspective.

Part 2 begins with a discussion of the political context of rural life, establishes the formal structures by which policies are enacted, reviews recent policy initiatives and developments, identifies relevant advisory bodies and non-government agencies who contribute to the social and policy context of rural work, and identifies useful sources of information and data which can be used to support planning and development. It then considers the case for a rural premium in the funding allocations made to rural services and identifies how some agencies are tackling this issue. Part 2 then goes on to indicate how users and workers may exert influence upon decision-making bodies and processes, and includes reference to practical examples of successful innovation. Finally, it reviews the practicalities and pitfalls of joint working and working with voluntary agencies, and points up some important issues in workforce support, and in different approaches to the evaluation of services.

It is worth noting that each agency, whether statutory or voluntary, plays a part in actively constructing particular ideas of what the countryside is, and what it might or should be like. This is often done unwittingly as agencies provide services without considering the broader picture of rural life which is supported or reinforced by their activities. By default, their activities often marginalise or ignore particular sections of rural society, and when they make plans or contribute to development activities, they often construct a vision of how things should be, in which their own perceptions are presumed to be normal, ordinary and self-evident. Consequently, discrimination is left unchallenged and the aims that are targeted represent the views of those who are socially and demographically dominant, and thus fail to consider the interests of those who are marginalised, unpopular, or relatively powerless. Perhaps the most common failings arise from the assumption that rural communities are homogenous entities with a common culture and common interests. How can this be so, when poverty often exists next door to comparative wealth or when minorities are subjected to social exclusion, vilification, and at best, often feel that acceptance of their existence in a community is contingent and conditional?

The Politics of the Countryside

In the UK, unlike many other European countries, the politics of the countryside have not played a major part in British political life, and as recently as 1995 even, a White Paper entitled *Rural England: A Nation Committed to a Living Countryside*, made only a fleeting mention of rural poverty by reference to low pay, unemployment and underemployment, and lack of access to services. However, after many years of neglect, the politics of the countryside are becoming the subject of debate at the highest levels of government, and this is evident in the increased attention given to rural issues such as BSE, genetic modification of foods, new roads and housing developments, the 'right to roam', and so on. Ilbery makes the point that:

> . . . *rural areas are now at the centre of interest and debate . . . and many of the processes of change stem from broader and more general socio-economic and political processes. As a consequence, policy makers are having to re-evaluate policies relating to 'rural space'.*

> (Ilbery, 1998, p1)

This renewed focus upon rural issues represents a significant change in British politics, for although the farming lobby has been quite effective in securing assistance and support over most of the post-war period, until recently neither the government or the wider public has shown much appreciation of the broader interests of the rural population. This lack of interest is in part a consequence of the relatively early urbanisation of

Britain, in that most people are several generations removed from any direct experience of living and working in the countryside. So for most people, for whom the countryside is not home, nor their place of work, and who have no direct links through their families, knowledge of the realities of rural life may be very limited.

It was noted earlier in Part 1 that many urban dwellers often have a sense of their own superiority in relation to those who live in the countryside. Ching and Creed (1997), contend that this form of cultural hierarchy is common throughout the world and that the assumption of superiority is often established in similar ways. For example, the common notion that rural folk do not really appreciate the countryside and simply see it as an economic resource to be exploited, is reinforced when country people react strongly to efforts to curtail their economic activities. In a similar fashion, country people are often presumed not to appreciate the beauty and worth of the countryside, nor to have any feelings for the animals they raise, and ultimately slaughter. Paradoxically, in direct contradiction to this assumption, many rural dwellers explicitly acknowledge that it is their appreciation of the beauty and the benefits of rural life that keeps them in the countryside. Some urbanites who ignore or deny the existence of such feelings amongst country people, use an 'environmental rhetoric (which) affirms the dominance of the urban perspective' (Ching and Creed, 1997, p21), and often discounts or oversimplifies the views of those who actually live in the countryside. Consequently, whether it arises from a lack of contact or from some position which devalues or derogates rural perspectives, the result is that the variety and complexity of rural politics is often reduced to a rather simplistic image of rural conservatism, or is quite simply ignored altogether.

The marginalisation of rural life has had other consequences. Although one should be wary of characterising the Countryside March upon London in 1998 and the subsequent demonstrations in 1999 as evidence of a coherent political movement or even a consensus of concerns, it nevertheless surprised many Westminster politicians and reminded them that there was a broader range of rural constituents who felt that their interests were not being addressed. However, it would be erroneous to assume that there is an homogenous and unified rural point of view that is represented by such protests. For example, while considerable media attention was focused upon the proposed ban on fox hunting as the stimulus for the protest, it is likely that this was not the primary concern of many of those who took part in the marches. For some, it represented an opportunity to remind the government that increases in fuel taxes aimed at reducing pollution bore disproportionately upon those who lived in the countryside, and that they often had no alternative but to use private motor cars. In fact, the marches mobilised a rather disparate range of organisations and interests, whose main common denominator was that they resided in the countryside rather than in towns and cities.

We should not assume that conservatism is an intrinsic quality of rural politics, but one that, as Ching and Creed contend, is *made*, particularly by 'reactionary members of the middle and upper classes seeking validation for their own more conservative views . . . (for) the marginality of rural people renders them vulnerable to conservative manoeuvring (1997, p29). The marches provide an almost perfect illustration of how rural interests can be mobilised by conservatives in resistance to proposed changes that would have little effect upon the majority of rural residents. So while the protest has been presented, and even possibly manipulated, by some groups to portray fox hunting as if it were a central feature of rural life, in reality it remains a relatively minority pursuit, and one whose economic importance, in terms of potential loss of employment and so on, is probably marginal when compared to farming and other rural industries. Indeed, the common assumption that the countryside is the 'natural' home of conservative politics relies upon a very selective reading of British politics. In particular, it ignores both the socialist and nationalist politics of Scotland and Wales, and the role that rural districts have played in these movements. The reality is that rural politics are often more complex than many commentators suppose. The countryside may often be the site where resistance to change appears to be endemic, or rather, where such apparent stability is often used in an idealised way to represent a mythical picture of British life and identity (see the discussion on symbolic representations of rurality and difference in Part 1), but at the same time, there may be strong independent or radical traditions which, in many respects, run counter to the expectations of outsiders. This complexity is seen in other European countries too. In France, for example, it is the countryside rather than the urban areas which have been the heartland of communist politics.

A more useful way of coming to terms with rural politics might be gained by appreciating two common features. First, rural politics is not easily amenable to simple generalisations, for there may be a world of difference between the concerns of people living in Wiltshire or Dorset, and those living in the marginal farming areas of Scotland or in small industrial villages on the declining coal fields of the north east of England, but this complexity is not evident because of the dominance of the party system. Second, that resistance to marginalisation is an enduring feature of rural politics, along with a resistance either to dominance by urban politicians or to the predominant political parties. Thus, a political pragmatism in terms of resistance to doctrinaire ideologies is commonplace, and 'maverick' politicians, even sometimes operating within the major political parties though more often running as 'independents', are not unusual in rural councils. It was noted in Part 1 that definitions of what is rural are a point of contention, and Halfacree has suggested that 'the quest for any single, all-embracing definition of the rural is neither desirable or feasible' (1993, p34). Nonetheless, people's ideas and decisions are influenced by their notions of what *they* think rural is. Consequently, the definitions espoused by policy makers may overlook some sorts of problems and deal only with those that are recognisable to them from their perspective, thereby ignoring the 'considerable exploitation and deprivation' (Ilbery, 1998, p4) suffered by others. The politics of the British countryside can be typified as having been:

- ignored or marginalised
- seen as a place for improvement and development, by assuming the superiority of the urban perspectives
- assumed to be a conservative heartland
- representing some notion of purity and stability in assertions of nationalism

Policy Making Structures and Processes

This section identifies the various bodies who have a duty or a role in providing and developing rural social services. It is written at a time when there are considerable changes proposed for local government structures, so as well as reflecting the current situation it outlines the direction of likely changes. Although this may seem a little confusing, it is useful to make a distinction between the sources of law which empower statutory social services, the structures through which local authorities exercise their duties, and the various non-governmental bodies which have a role in the social development of the countryside.

Statutory authorities and responsibilities

Despite the plethora of changes in policy and structures, the main piece of legislation which empowers local authorities in the provision of social services in England and Wales remains the 1970 Local Authority Social Services Act. This Act specifies the functions that local authorities must undertake and requires them to have a social services committee and to appoint a Director of Social Services. While the basic functions and responsibilities have been extended and modified by government policy directives and subsequent specific legislation, such as the National Health Service and Community Care Act (1990) and the Children Act (1989), the underpinning legislation remains the 1970 Act, and there are no current proposals to change this. However, the statutory framework of local authorities has changed several times since then, most notably in the:

- Local Government Act (1972) which removed Country Borough Councils
- Local Government Act (1985) which abolished the Greater London Council and the Metropolitan County Councils
- Local Government Act (1992) which developed the structure of unitary authorities (discussed in more detail later in this section)

In Northern Ireland, Scotland and Wales, additional changes to the administrative framework have taken place since devolution, most notably the transfer of functions from the Scottish Office and the Welsh Office to the Scottish Executive and the Office of the National Assembly for Wales. The situation in Northern Ireland is less certain, where powers were devolved to the Northern Ireland Executive in December 1999, suspended in February 2000 and reconvened in June 2000. Further changes to the way in which local authorities conduct their business and organise the responsibility for local services were proposed in the 1998 White Paper, *Modern Local Government: In Touch With the People*. This White Paper aims to improve the responsiveness and the effectiveness of the political management of local government and to revive local interest in local democracy. There has been particular concern about the low levels of voter participation in local elections, currently running at an average of 40 per cent, and the lack of strategic planning within council committees. Several models of how a local authority may operate are proposed, and these include a directly elected mayor with a cabinet, a cabinet with a leader, and a directly elected mayor with a council manager. The proposals also include the establishment of a *Best Value Inspectorate* and the identification of *beacon councils* who will exemplify best practice in efficiency and responsiveness to local needs. If these proposals are enacted then one result will be greater diversity in the ways that local government is run, and consequently, in how social services are managed and overseen within local authorities. For example, the old-style social services committees might be replaced by a decentralised system of area committees, which may enhance the prospect of more responsive rural social services.

The 1992 Local Government Act in England and Wales, followed by the reorganisation of local government (LGR) in Scotland, has had marked effects upon the provision of social services in rural areas, particularly in Scotland and Wales. The setting up of unitary authorities, responsible for the whole range of services within their area, has reduced the size and scope of some of the former shire counties in England and Wales. As Craig and

Manthorpe note, 'the overall effect has been to triple the number of local authorities responsible for social services provision in areas where reorganisation occurred' (1999, p2). In many areas it led to larger urban districts becoming separate from the 'rump' authorities which now cover the remaining predominantly rural areas. In some instances, agreements between authorities continue to make services accessible for rural dwellers who live on the margins of the new urban authority districts, but in others, the rural authorities have not always been able to replace services that were formerly available to residents.

LGR has also reduced the scope for economies of scale and economies of specialisation as many of the smaller unitary authorities are now too small to reap the benefits formerly available to larger units. This was most noticeable in Wales, where twenty-two unitary authorities replaced the previous six authorities that had responsibility for social services. Consequently, many social services departments have struggled to match previous levels of service and maintain pre-existing commitments to service users. Areas of activity that are perceived as marginal to the immediate tasks of delivering services have often been subjected to severe cuts. Training units, for example, struggled to maintain their in-house provision and have found it difficult to participate fully in collaborative arrangements with other authorities and providers of training, such as those required for the Diploma in Social Work and Approved Social Worker (Mental Health Act). Furthermore, in some authorities these changes, together with the dearth of resources, seemed to lead to a state of permanent reorganisation, as social service departments were restructured once and then often reorganised again. This was particularly damaging to staff morale and led to a loss of expertise among those employed and those local politicians who had an interest in social services (Craig and Manthorpe, 1999).

The introduction of LGR also coincided with policy changes in regard to competitive tendering, private finance, and charging for services, and this has led to a greater reliance upon the independent sector of charitable voluntary, and profit-seeking organisations. For many voluntary organisations, LGR severely disrupted the relationships they had established with social service departments and often led to funding problems as contracts were renegotiated and grants reduced or ended completely. Craig and Manthorpe's research showed that many voluntary sector bodies were marginalised and cut-off from information. Moreover:

Although many voluntary organisations saw themselves as representing users' interests ... (they) ... were often left with difficult decisions as to when and how to communicate the consequences of change to users and carers groups.
(Craig and Manthorpe, 1999, p5)

Voluntary organisations were often required to respond to new developments with little warning or opportunity for adequate preparation, and in most cases without any additional funding to cover these changes. Many users only found out about changes to their services, such as changes in charging policies, from reports in the local media.

Reorganisation, however, did provide an opportunity to re-examine service policy and provision, and to consider whether there were more appropriate ways of meeting local needs. In authorities where this opportunity was fully exploited there have been considerable changes in the financial devolution and operational dispersal of services. For example, in Wiltshire there has been a decentralisation and localisation of community care services into smaller area teams with their own operational and purchasing budgets (Social Services Inspectorate, 1998b). Furthermore, having coterminous administrative districts for housing and social services can enable better strategic planning when both responsibilities are housed within the same local authority. The government has been positive about these moves and, as noted earlier, the proposals for local government modernisation are clearly intended to promote such changes. The underlying assumption is that more localness will promote more responsive services, and while there is some basis for optimism in regard to rural services, it is too early to draw any firm conclusions. Indeed, it would be erroneous to assume that such changes will solve some of the problems which face users and providers of services. Resource shortages will remain an important factor, and there are also grounds for concern in regard to provision for minority groups. This point, namely, that we should be wary of an uncritical acceptance of localisation, is one which I have noted elsewhere in regard to devolution in the UK:

> *In fact, for some groups, such as disability activists, devolution could dissipate their efforts and subsequent influence. While a larger society may have good reasons to recognise and incorporate particular interests, smaller, more homogenous ones may be less inclined to recognise these differences. If this were to happen ... (it) might result in greater inequities than those under current arrangements.*
>
> (Pugh and Thompson, 1999, p27)

It is possible that after localisation it might be even more difficult than it currently is to make satisfactory provision for minority groups, and especially for unpopular groups such as travellers and asylum seekers. Local government modernisation and the continuing development of the devolved powers of the Welsh and Northern Ireland Assemblies and the Scottish Parliament are likely to further stimulate the trend towards decentralisation in policy making and the organisation of service delivery. Although the question of worker influence on service development is addressed later in this section, it is worth noting here, that increased localisation can increase pressures upon local workers who may feel more exposed and vulnerable when working and making their contribution within smaller communities (Martinez-Brawley, 1991; Yanay, 1989).

Policy initiatives and developments

Many reports into levels of social service provision have indicated that there are marked disparities in the likelihood of country dwellers receiving comparable services to those living in urban areas (Spilsbury and Lloyd, 1998; Department of Health, 1996; Hayle, 1996). Yet, as the Social Services Inspectorate point out:

> . . . *providing services to people in rural areas does not happen in a policy and practice vacuum . . . almost all social care legislation, regulation and policy guidance from central government applies to people and services no matter what their geography.*
>
> (SSI, 1999b, p11)

The reasons for these disparities are complex. Some arise from the higher costs associated with providing rural services, some come from ignorance about the extent of needs, while others stem from a lack of good information about what social services are actually provided within different areas of the UK. Fortunately, recent policy initiatives may begin to address these disparities and perhaps provide the first steps in remedying the inequities that follow from them. The general move towards specifying aims and targets, identifying performance indicators and establishing the true costs of service provision, all have the potential to point up the problematic assumptions and practices that hinder the development of fairer and more effective rural social services. The White Papers on modernising local government and social services, the recommendations arising from the McIntosh Commission in Scotland, and the new regional *Commissions for Care Standards*, are indicative of the government's drive for efficiency, accountability, transparency, and better strategic planning in local services. The Local Government Act (1999) requires local authorities in England and Wales to seek *Best Value* in their operations, and this is defined as the duty to secure continuous 'improvement in the exercise of all functions . . . having regard to a combination of economy, efficiency and effectiveness' (HMSO, 1999, p2). Thus local authorities, not just in social services, will be required to:

- Inform local people of the performance objectives and targets they have set for their services.
- Provide local people with a summary of their performance in meeting the previous year's objectives and targets.
- Publish this information in a Local Performance Plan which will be audited independently.
- Review all of their services within five years.

Furthermore, in addition to the stipulation that local authorities have publicly accessible service plans with specified targets for service provision and development, the Act also requires that local authorities consult with employees and users when preparing service plans. The *Best Value* initiative also includes performance indicators for services, which are intended to focus local authorities' attention upon aspects of service that the government sees as national priorities. These indicators include:

- emergency psychiatric readmission
- re-registrations on the child protection register
- admissions of supported residents aged 18–64 to residential/nursing care
- ethnicity of people receiving assessment
- ethnicity of adults receiving services
- assessments leading to provision of service

A further level of scrutiny will be provided by the Audit Commission (England and Wales) who will inspect local authorities and check that reviews have taken place and that the performance targets are sufficiently challenging to secure real improvements in services. Where serious deficiencies are revealed, the decision on what sort of intervention might be needed will be made by the appropriate government minister in the different countries. In extreme cases, this could include directly taking over responsibility for the function/s of the local authority. Thus far in Scotland, there is no statutory requirement underpinning *Best Value*, though it is possible that legislation may be enacted to this effect. Nevertheless, the same broad aims are being pursued by the Scottish Executive and all local authorities are participating in its efforts to develop the initiative.

It would be tempting to assume that improvements in rural services will follow from this drive for specificity and transparency, but it is no exaggeration to say that many departments are reeling under the weight of this onslaught of modernisation. Social service departments are having to respond to a welter of other policy developments including—*Quality Protects, Sure Start, National Priorities Guidance, Better Government for Older*

People, and so on, and the Association of Directors of Social Services have expressed concerns about this. One director was quoted as saying, 'the criticisms are mounting up because directors feel so inundated that they can take no more. Local government reorganisation has created lots of small authorities and there are no banks of people at the ready to implement the policies (Hirst, 1999, p20). Unsurprisingly, hard-pressed departments often take the line of least resistance, and there is some evidence emerging that the *Best Value* initiative, which replaced Compulsory Competitive Tendering but did not abolish contracting out, is being interpreted primarily in financial terms with quality being very much a secondary consideration. Thus, compliance is seen to be achieved most easily by simply contracting services out to cheaper independent sector providers (Hirst, 1999). The daunting scale of the demands currently being made upon social service departments can be seen in just one area of practice. For example, workers in mental health services have had to get to grips with the implications of—*Building Bridges; Still Building Bridges* (sic); *Partnership in Action;* the development of *Framework* plans; the review of the *Mental Health Act;* and a revised *Code of Practice.* All this, as well as begin to come to terms with the impact of the *European Convention on Human Rights* and the *Human Rights Act 1998*, upon their practice.

Advisory bodies, non-government agencies and fora

There is a plethora of different agencies with responsibilities for advising, developing and supporting policy and practice in rural areas, and it is likely that many social workers are unaware, or possibly confused, about the different bodies and their respective remits. Therefore, the aim of this section is to briefly identify the main organisations and to give some indication about which of their activities have relevance for those seeking to develop social services.

In England, until April 1999, the Rural Development Commission (RDC) was a government funded agency which commissioned many valuable surveys of rural life and provided much useful information about the problems and needs of rural people. Its brief was very wide and encompassed two primary roles. The first was to develop the rural economy and employment opportunities. The second was to promote community development, through a diverse range of activities, which included:

> ... *the provision of housing; support of rural services; encouragement and sponsorship of economic and social surveys and research; publicity, lobbying and information collection and dissemination; and support for the Rural Development of the NCVOs and the independent Rural Community Councils.*
>
> (Robinson, 1998, p284)

However, in 1999 the RDC was merged with the Countryside Commission to form the new Countryside Agency and this wider social brief has been carried into the new agency, which is 'responsible for advising the government and others, as well as taking action, on issues relating to the social economic and environmental well-being of the English countryside' (Gunner, 1999, p37). Among its other aims, it is explicitly charged with promoting social equity and economic opportunities for those who live in rural areas and it will continue to commission research, fund practical projects, and attempt to influence local and national government. It is anticipated that the Countryside Agency will continue the work of the RDC in providing an invaluable source of information for developing services, as well as being a direct funder of new projects. The main responsibility for economic development now lies with Regional Development Agencies, but they also distribute some funds for regeneration work.

Most areas of the UK have Rural Community Councils, or equivalent organisations such as the County Voluntary Councils in Wales, which are independent organisations whose core funding usually comes from national government via an intermediary organisation such as the Countryside Agency in England, or the Wales Council for Voluntary Action. Although additional funding may also come from local authorities, these councils usually rely upon lottery funding and other grants for specific projects. Community councils have two basic roles—to support other voluntary agencies in their work, and to promote the voice of local people to other bodies. They act as a channel of communication between those who use services and the statutory and voluntary organisations who provide them. The scope of their activities varies widely, but is aimed at community development and support. This typically includes, co-ordinating community transport schemes like Dial-a-Car community car services and Wheels-2-Work schemes which provide mopeds to help young people access work opportunities, good neighbour schemes to provide assistance with shopping and gardening, carers support schemes, information about services, and the provision of small grants. Some community councils work with other bodies to seek European Union funding for the regeneration of rural communities, and some undertake research to establish the extent of problems and unmet needs. Most community councils are linked at a national level by umbrella organisations like the Scottish Council for Voluntary Organisations, Action with Rural Communities in England, the Federation of Rural Community Councils or the National Council for Voluntary Organisations in England. These umbrella organisations provide direct support to their members and represent their views to government. They are an important clearing house for information about rural initiatives and are often important facilitators for those seeking to develop rural projects. Many of the major voluntary sector organisations have recognised that rural communities have not always been well-served by their activities and increasingly these bodies, together with other umbrella organisations, have begun to develop their own research, policies and projects, aimed at addressing the shortcomings they have identified. These organisations have a valuable contribution to make to the development of rural services, and they can often represent ideas and opinions that statutory bodies find difficult to access. Their role is discussed in more detail later in Part 2.

In Wales, the prime responsibility for economic development formerly lay with the Welsh Development Agency, which in 1998 was merged with the Development Board for Rural Wales and the Land Authority for Wales, and a new Welsh Development Agency now has a wider remit which includes the social development of rural communities where it fulfils a role rather similar to the old RDC in England. Currently, other funding for small rural development schemes is distributed by the Office of the National Assembly directly to eligible local authorities under the Local Authority Rural Scheme. The eligible bodies are the six authorities who also qualified for European funding, plus Wrexham. However, there is a possibility that this direct additional funding might in future be distributed through a local regeneration fund administered by the Office of the National Assembly. In 1998 a new advisory forum was created entitled the Rural Partnership for Wales. The forum is chaired by the Assembly Secretary for Agriculture and Rural Development and has the brief of enabling a wider range of organisations, including social care bodies and the Wales Council for Voluntary Action, to contribute to the future development of rural policies and programmes in Wales. Practitioners and service providers who seek to identify and establish needs, or to evaluate innovations in practice, can apply to WORD, the former Welsh Office of Research and Development, who have several schemes for awarding small research grants.

In Scotland, there is no direct equivalent to either the Countryside Agency or the Welsh Development Agency, as Scottish Enterprise, which covers the region from the Grampians to the Borders has a fairly narrow economic focus, though some of its work supports social development. The situation in the far north and the isles is rather different, and here, the Highlands and Islands Enterprise Network has a broader remit which does include social aims. Otherwise the responsibility for social development lies directly with local authorities or is partly advanced through the functions of other agencies such as Scottish Homes, which has a duty to promote social housing, and the Crofters Commission. However, it is possible that as the Scottish Parliament continues to develop the policies and structures through which it operates, further developments may lead to significant changes in the ways in which social development is promoted and enhanced in rural areas. In Northern Ireland, the main body promoting rural development is the Department of Agriculture and Rural Development, which, together with the Rural Development Council and the Rural Community Network, orchestrates and co-ordinates the Rural Development Programme. This programme brings together voluntary and statutory agencies and has a wide remit, including both social and economic aspects of rural life. For example, one element of its work focuses on the regeneration and redevelopment of fishing villages.

Information and planning data

Though the prime responsibility for marshalling data is one that social workers can expect to be undertaken elsewhere in their agencies, usually in a planning section or chief executive's department, they will sometimes need to get basic information and data in order to:

- better understand the nature of the community they work in
- reveal the extent of unmet needs
- determine the extent of existing provision
- contribute to better planning and development
- shape their own interventions
- form their own views about situations
- persuade and initiate action by other people

As few workers are likely to have either the resources or the skills necessary to collect and analyse data they need to know something of the extent of information collected by other organisations and how to access it. This section identifies some of the most useful sources and indicates some of the ways in which social workers and their departments might develop their own sources. Unfortunately, many social workers work in organisations where the top-down distribution of information is very much the norm. Of course, they form their own perceptions of what 'life is really like' as they go about their daily duties, but there is often no expectation that they will contribute to the collection and distribution of information and data within the agency. This leaves them vulnerable to misinformation, disinformation, and ill-prepared for a truly professional practice.

Perhaps the most useful basic information tool is access to the Internet. Most of the numerous government web sites can be accessed via *www.open.gov.uk* and this gives access to many useful sources, such as the text of all legislation since 1996 (*www.hmso.gov.uk*), briefing papers and policy documents aimed at local government (*www.detr.gov.uk*) and information specific to the constituent countries of the UK (*www.wales.gov.uk* for Wales, *www.scotland.gov.uk* for Scotland, and *www.northernireland.gov.uk* for

Northern Ireland). The Local Government Association has a useful site for information about the implementation of new developments, and also has good links to other organisations *(www.lganet.gov.uk)*. The Rowntree Foundation sponsors a large amount of research which is relevant to social work practice generally, and also has useful reports on rural problems and services *(www.jrf.org.uk)*. Finally, there are two academic gateways to social work and social sciences, which contain a wealth of information and have extensive links to other relevant web sites, based at the Universities of Bath and Southampton *(www.sosig.ac.uk)* and *(www.soton.ac.uk)*.

The Office of National Statistics (ONS), and many local authorities conduct surveys and censuses which are publicly accessible and can provide a surprising amount of detailed information. The ONS publishes an *Annual Abstract of Statistics* which summarises the wealth of data that is collected about British society and this is often a good starting point for getting an idea of what sorts of information are available. ONS also produces the *Population Census* every ten years and provides a further set of detailed Small Area Statistics (SAS) for every area of the UK and these are available from data archives at the University of Essex *(www.essex.ac.uk)*. This information is usually free and can be transferred in computer files, rather than in paper form. The quarterly journal *Population Trends* published by ONS is another good source of specialist information, as it publishes much of the continuing work that is done on analysing the Census data, as well as reporting the results of other social and economic surveys.

Other government departments can be a good source of information and the Office of the National Assembly in Wales and the Scottish Executive are both exceptionally helpful sources for these two countries. The Department of the Environment, Transport and the Regions' *Better Information* strategy is currently developing better information on how poverty, unemployment, crime and poor health affect different neighbourhoods to assist those who are involved in renewal projects, the aim being 'to provide communities, Government and front-line workers with unprecedented levels of information about where they live' (DETR, 2000, p1). Although this strategy will largely focus upon urban areas, it is likely that it will provide a model which will be used more widely in planning and developing services. Some local authorities conduct their own censuses, and many commission small scale studies which focus upon particular issues, population projections, particular localities, household surveys, and rural facilities. Housing departments and housing associations can be useful sources especially on the demographic profile of needs in particular areas, as housing need is often a good indicator of other social problems. Over the last few years it has become increasingly obvious that many providers of social services do not have reliable information about the communities they are supposed to serve, and it is interesting to note that the *Best Value* initiative requires local authorities to collect more extensive information. In addition, the Social Services Inspectorate has recommended that all social service departments make a local audit of the services that are available locally, and include within this, those provided by independent sector organisations.

There are numerous examples of projects undertaking their own research, but three that are of particular interest because they demonstrate a clear focus on equal opportunity issues are noted here. Craig and his colleagues (1999), described how research undertaken by the Lincolnshire Forum for Racial Justice 'revealed the inadequacy of the local database for researching the needs of minority ethnic groups' (in Henderson and Kaur, 1999, p29) because it undercounted the actual numbers of people from ethnic minorities in the area. They used a questionnaire to establish what relevant services already existed, an approach also used by the Rural Race Equality Project in south-west England (Dhalech, 1999). Hooper's (1996), study of a self-help initiative for lone parents in Yorkshire and Humberside showed how the primary need was established with reference to census data, which indicated that there were 3,381 lone parent households who were potentially isolated or in need of some help and support.

One way of gathering information about communities which social workers may not be aware of is parish appraisal, which Moseley describes as 'arguably now the most significant single tool of community development in contemporary rural Britain' (1997, p197). Since 1970 over 1,500 English, Welsh and some Scottish rural communities 'have systematically taken stock of themselves and their future' (Moseley, 1997, p197). Of course, the fact that parish appraisals are a tool of community development precludes most social workers from having experience of them, simply because their professional role does not usually encompass community development. Parish appraisals, however, do have something to contribute to the planning of personal social services, as they are the means by which a community can identify for itself particular local characteristics, problems, needs, and opportunities. Appraisal is usually undertaken by means of a questionnaire, but it can also use other development tools, such as local fora, public meetings, education initiatives and so on. Moseley suggests that a parish appraisal usually takes a year to complete, and he identifies nine typical stages of development:

- establishing local support for an appraisal
- forming a steering group to consider what to appraise, and how to appraise it

- planning the survey and designing the questionnaire
- distributing and collecting the information
- analysing the information
- drafting a report summarising the findings and any recommendations
- distributing the report and organising local discussion of the report to establish a mandate for further action
- undertaking the action, and finally
- evaluating and monitoring the outcomes

Parish appraisals may be initiated by a range of bodies, and may be undertaken in communities of widely differing sizes, but wherever they originate, the crucial point is that these stages are 'owned' and managed by the local community, although they may be assisted in undertaking the appraisal by other agencies and professionals. Moseley states that:

The scope of the appraisal and, hence, the coverage of the appraisal report, varies from place to place ... Typically, they embrace the parish's demographic and social structure, its housing conditions, environment, transport and accessibility, employment, service provision, social activities etc.

(Moseley, 1997, p199)

While the outcomes of many appraisals are not always relevant to providers of social services, often being more concerned with transport, local enterprise, footpaths, recreational needs and so on, there is no reason why they should not provide useful information. If service organisations are able to have some input into the design of the survey in terms of the sorts of issues that are explored, they can help to set the agenda for the research, and in doing so, begin a process that can alert a community to problems that might otherwise go unrecognised, or receive little sympathetic consideration. Of course, statutory social service departments should be wary of over-influencing the development of the survey, or of appearing to 'take over' the project, nor should they use their involvement in such projects as an excuse not to carry out direct research of their own. Nevertheless, a parish appraisal provides a unique opportunity to find out what a particular community feels about existing provision and about what it needs.

A successful appraisal can provide the basis for partnership with local groups and provide opportunities to build upon the potential of existing resources within a community, but more importantly, it may galvanise a community into its own actions and its own responses to particular issues or problems. An appraisal may be a means to an end, in terms of the provision of information, but it can also become an end in itself, as participation in the processes may increase the social and political capabilities of individuals and groups within a community, and therefore generate a more confident and assertive community. Finally, the involvement of social service agencies in appraisals may not only help to form the basis of future forms of partnership, but it may also help to develop a broader understanding of the complexities and problems that face service providers. It can help to 'legitimise' some of the inevitable conflicts which agencies face as they try to reconcile resources with needs, and can provide a better political platform for statutory agencies to undertake their responsibilities. Further information about parish appraisal can be obtained from most rural community councils in England, from the South Pembrokeshire Partnership for Action with Rural Communities (SPARC), the 'Jigso' campaign in Wales, and from the Rural Forum in Scotland.

Rural Costs and Rural Premiums

The obvious reasons for the increased costs associated with rural services arise from the reduced opportunities for economies of scale, higher transport costs, and the reduced rural infrastructure, but there are also some underpinning assumptions which contribute to this relative disadvantage. For example, a study by Help the Aged (1996), found that the overall expenditure per elderly person in rural districts was less than half of that provided in urban areas, and a later study indicated some of the reasons for this:

> *Less money is made available for older people who live in rural areas . . . because it is assumed (rather than based on fact) that . . . (they) are less likely to need help, and that the amount needed for their care will be lower. Smaller proportions of older people are expected to need social services help in rural areas than elsewhere; and local authorities in rural areas are expected to spend significantly less on social services for older people than other types of authority.*
> (Pizey and Lyon, 1998, p12)

The case for a rural premium to reflect the higher costs of delivering services in rural areas has been championed by a number of bodies. The National Council for Voluntary Organisations has consistently sought to establish the case for it (NCVO, 1994; Woollett, 1993), and two reports for the Rural Development Commission (Hayle, 1996; 1998), demonstrated that existing funding mechanisms for allocating resources to public services disadvantaged rural populations.

Research undertaken by the County Councils Network found that the Standard Spending Assessment (SSA) for shire counties was consistently lower than the average of all English authorities. For example:

- 'the SSA for a child at risk in Cumbria was 77 per cent of the average for England
- the SSA for domiciliary care in Dorset was 82 per cent of the average for England
- the SSA for elderly residential care in North Yorkshire was 77 per cent of the average for England'

(Shropshire County Council, 2000, p3)

Part of the problem is that most of the factors that are used in the formulae for calculating funding allocations to local government are linked to population density and these, fail to adequately reflect rural costs. Thus, while population sparsity is included as a relevant factor, there is probably an insufficient weighting given to it. Studies undertaken by the University of York indicate that for domiciliary care the additional cost element in a rural area is about 20 per cent (1998), and Shropshire Social Services have undertaken some preliminary research which indicates that for home care staff, travel time as a percentage of contact hours varies from 11.05 per cent in the least rural area, to 18.51 per cent in the most rural district (Shropshire County Council, 2000). The additional costs of providing rural services also bear upon non-statutory agencies too. A Social Services Inspectorate report into rural community care services found that some providers experienced similar difficulties to the voluntary sector agencies especially in regard to transport costs, with some 'providers claiming to be servicing rural areas at a loss for fear of losing the block contract' (1999b, p10). The Most Sparsely Populated Counties Group (MSPCG) of local authorities examined the differences that existed between services, and frustration at central government's reluctance to remedy the inequities of current funding mechanisms has led some authorities to make considerable efforts to establish the case for a rural premium. For example, a coalition of local government bodies in Shropshire, whose members included the health and police authorities formed a working group to explore the issues and make the case for increased funding for their public services (Shropshire Regeneration Partnerships, 1998). Their key messages to the government were, that:

- Many people in rural areas do not have equality of access to services.
- There is a significant 'rural premium' on the costs of providing public services in rural areas which is not adequately recognised.
- Many people in rural areas are now paying disproportionately more in tax for less in services.
- There is inconsistency in the way that government includes consideration of rurality in making funding allocations to different public

services. For example, additional money is made available to the fire service but not to social services.

The coalition assembled an impressive range of information to support their case that rural services were more costly to deliver and that spending caps imposed over the previous years had disproportionately impacted upon their capacity to provide effective and fair services. They showed, for instance, that 84 per cent of parishes had no daily bus service, and also used data drawn from the Rural Development Commission to show that they had 522 settlements with populations of less than 2,000 which made up 25 per cent of the county's population, and that 442 of these actually had less than 200 people living in them, but still comprised 10 per cent of the county's population. They also used income data to demonstrate the inequities in taxation in relation to low local earnings. So whereas a person living in London or one of the metropolitan counties would on average need to work around 1.32 or 1.33 weeks to pay their council tax, in Shropshire the average was 1.81 weeks.

Unfortunately, they were unsuccessful in their efforts to attract more funding, but signs that government attitudes to this issue are slowly changing are evident in the Department of Health report entitled *Developing Health and Social Care in Rural England* (1996), and more recently, in the report, *Care in the Country* (1999), which summed up the current situation in regard to rural communities, thus:

> ... services, information and facilities are more expensive and/or difficult to access than in urban areas. This can mean they are less likely to be used, leading to a breakdown in provision. It can also mean that people in rural communities have lower expectations regarding the quality of services and this obliges them to be more self-sufficient, particularly in terms of self-help.
>
> (Social Services Inspectorate, 1999, p2)

In a related development, the Department of the Environment and the Welsh Assembly have commissioned a review of the Index of Deprivation used to measure the scale of deprivation in different communities. Currently, this work, undertaken by Michael Noble at Oxford University, is proposing to reduce the numbers of indicators from twelve to six—income, work, health, education, housing and most significant, geographical access to services. The outcome of this exercise is likely to be that rural communities will fare better in subsequent grant allocations as their position in the overall ranking of deprivation in communities worsens. While central government may yet have to fully recognise the case for a rural premium, it is clear that local social services should do so, but the extent to which they internally formalise rurality as a factor in distributing resources is unclear. The Social Services Inspectorate noted with approval that Wiltshire had introduced a rural premium into its formulae for distributing budgets to local teams, albeit a rather meagre 3 per cent uplift (1998b). Certainly, those authorities linked to the County Councils Network have begun to grapple with the difficulty of defining performance criteria which adequately reflect the complexity of rural location and social disadvantage.

The Shropshire coalition of public service providers did, however, provide a helpful framework for categorising the problems facing providers and users of their services. They typified them as:

- Services available at a level broadly similar across the area, but where the nature of delivery may show a distinct rural pattern which would impose additional costs upon the provider, e.g. meals on wheels transportation and home care.
- Services where there is distinct and measurable reduction in the level provided, e.g. day care for older people and adults with learning disabilities.
- Services which people can only access by travelling and incurring their own costs to receive the service, e.g. day care, alcohol and drugs rehabilitation.
- Services where discretionary charges are levied at levels above the average, e.g. concessionary fare eligibility, day care charges.
- Services which are not available at all because of the potential user's location.
- Services where, because of rural isolation, it becomes necessary to provide a more expensive form of service rather than none at all or service at a reduced level, e.g. admission to residential services rather than home care.

The value of this categorisation is that it helps us to characterise current levels and forms of service provision without having to go into the detail of what is specifically problematic about a particular service, and thus not only describes the situation but focuses attention upon the main issues in terms of equity and so makes the implications of decisions about services very clear. Finally, there is one other aspect worth noting, which is that population 'thresholds' commonly militate against services in rural areas because minima, such as class sizes in schools, or levels of need, do not reach the points that trigger intervention, or more commonly, result in the increasing centralisation of some services. Although infrastructure costs such as transport, travelling time, and accommodation can contribute greatly to the cost of providing services in rural areas, as we shall see later, these are areas where there is some scope for efficiency gains providing that agencies are willing to be creative and flexible in the ways in which they deliver services. Unfortunately, if models of how a service should operate remain resolutely urban, then it will always be difficult to respond effectively to local needs and local opportunities.

Influencing Policy and Service Development

One of the central features of social services work is that needs are often essentially subjective perceptions of what is absent, inadequate, or unsatisfactory in a given situation. Social service agencies have difficulty in deciding how best to meet needs when there is potentially such a degree of individual subjectivity in establishing which elements are most significant in a person's situation. The standard means of reducing subjectivity is to use some assessment protocol or instrument, such as a questionnaire or rating scale. Such devices are clearly useful in trying to develop an equitable response to often very different situations, and of course, they enable agencies to ration scarce resources in what seems to them a defensible manner. However, there is a fundamental problem inherent in these types of procedures, namely, that the construction of the assessment device presupposes certain features of need, and omits or under-emphasises other features, and this selectivity may be exacerbated by the ways in which they are used. For example, a study of older peoples' housing needs by Midgely et al. found that:

> *Older people are restricted in how they can express their needs when being assessed. A primary cause of this is the nature of the assessment process: the questions that are asked are largely determined by resource availability and current spending priorities. Older people are not encouraged to articulate needs and wishes that cannot currently be provided for, and may not receive an assessment at all if it is known in advance (through an informal pre-assessment screening) that they do not qualify for a service.*

> (Midgley et al., 1997, p2)

Regardless of the area of service, the upshot of this mode of operation is that social work becomes a service-led enterprise rather than a needs-led one, and client's needs not only go unmet, but may also go unrecognised. In such circumstances it becomes impossible to develop useful services, and when attempts are made to evaluate the effectiveness of the services, the methodology and the criteria that are used frequently pre-empt the conclusions. Therefore, it is axiomatic that service development must involve actual and potential users of the services, otherwise what is offered may be inadequate, or simply irrelevant to people's needs.

User perspectives and participation

The case for user involvement in the development of social services is well established in an academic sense (Beresford and Croft, 1993; Braye and Preston-Shoot, 1995; Jordan, 1997; Oliver, 1996), and is increasingly becoming enshrined in legislation and policy guidance, but arguably it remains a rarity in most practice. This section presumes the desirability of user participation and does not seek to establish the general case for it, though a rationale does emerge from the discussion. Instead, the focus is directed towards how it might be sought in the rural context.

An evaluation of projects that attempted to enhance service user input to the planning and commissioning of services for people with disabilities undertaken by Lindow (1999), made somewhat depressing reading. It found that:

- Many commissioners of services were still unaware of basic means of facilitating user involvement, such as access to buildings, the provision of information in appropriate and alternative formats, eg, Braille, large type, minority languages, and so on.
- Many commissioners had little idea of how cultural and religious needs might affect the involvement of people from minority ethnic communities.
- Service users tended to be involved at the more general level of planning and not at the point where decisions about commissioning particular services were being made.
- Commissioners sometimes failed to realise how long it took to set up effective means of consultation before user involvement could proceed.
- Disabled people often believed that commissioners needed training in order to involve service users more fully, although the commissioners themselves did not always think that they did!
- Commissioners felt that as they bore the legal responsibility for making decisions, they should do this alone.

However, there were some more positive findings which supported the experience of other projects. Specifically, that:

- When given training and support service users could be effectively involved in planning and decision making.
- Outreach workers were an effective means of contacting users from more marginalised groups, and personal contact was more effective than letters and leaflets.
- Employing experienced user consultants can usefully increase the involvement of other users providing that they develop a partnership

77

approach with other local organisations of disabled people, and providing that there are systems to carry the work on afterwards.

The training of service users to prepare them for effective involvement should, according to Lindow (1999), include assertiveness and 'speaking up' courses, preferably run by other service users, guidance on purchasers' and providers' decision making structures, training in committee procedures and negotiating skills, equal opportunities and legal rights training, and information about what has, and what has not worked in other areas.

Powys Mental Health Alliance (PMHA) developed a very practical approach to the empowerment of relatively isolated and powerless users of mental health services in rural areas (Pugh and Richards, 1996). PMHA is an informal countywide network of individuals and groups with an interest in mental health issues. It operates in a large rural area of approximately 75×35 miles, with a low population density, and it attempts to develop and sustain a voice for otherwise isolated, sometimes unconfident, and often marginalised people, so that they may contribute effectively to the evaluation and development of local mental health services. The Alliance has established an approach to reviewing services which overcomes several of the main obstacles to user involvement in rural areas, namely distance and transport difficulties, and lack of experience and confidence in elucidating and stating their views.

Their approach was to organise a series of one-day events over a ten week period at eight different locations. The venues were selected to provide a pleasant environment in a location with good road connections and to maximise access by public transport. Typically, these were hotels or inns in small market town centres. To promote maximum participation, crèches were provided, transport expenses paid, special diets were catered for, and considerable effort was put into publicising the events by local voluntary groups, home aides, and mental health workers. Consequently, over 130 people participated in the events. They did not have to record their attendance, and several preferred not to do so, because they felt that this further safeguarded their anonymity. Each event was facilitated by service users, who had previously attended a day workshop organised by Wales MIND. The training used discussion and role plays and focused upon how to provide introductions and help people feel comfortable, how to enhance participation and keep some overall structure to the group events, how to undertake the differing roles of scribe and facilitator, how to cope with distress and with other typical problems, such as conflicts, or overly dominant participants who monopolised discussion, and so on. At the events, the facilitators worked in pairs, one as a scribe—recording the discussion, and the other as the facilitator—who introduced and guided the group sessions. The facilitators received a small payment for their work and nearly always worked outside of their own 'home' areas. The PMHA development worker attended the venues to provide advice and support to the facilitators, and to deal with any other problems that arose, but did not attend the group sessions nor play any part in any of the discussions.

The morning sessions were relatively unstructured, allowing free discussion and exchange of views on a wide range of subjects. The issues that aroused most concern included the question of informed choice of treatment and medication, clear and accessible information about services and benefits, how the process of hospitalisation was managed, the unresponsiveness and attitudes of GPs and other professionals, stigma and public attitudes, support for carers, and transport difficulties. A particular concern was that help was often not forthcoming until a crisis had occurred. The afternoon sessions focused upon four questions:

- What would help to prevent a crisis in your life?
- What would be helpful during a crisis?
- What would be helpful in 'recovery'?
- What would be helpful to maintain stability in your life?

The groups' responses to the questions were remarkably congruent, very focused, and provided important information about user's preferences. For example, responses to the first question included the provision of a telephone at home, a 24-hour help line and round the clock access to local social workers, continuity of workers from hospital to community, counselling and access to advocacy, and practical help at home with things like housework, shopping and child care. Responses to the other questions included alternatives to hospital, counselling support, temporary foster care places for children, better aftercare support plans and help with the practicalities of returning home, befriending schemes, and more public health education on mental health problems. Most participants were appreciative of the opportunity to express their views and to meet with other service users, and the facilitators were also very positive in their feedback too. The information was summarised in a report that was widely circulated to service planners and providers, and the information was also used by user representatives on planning fora who felt empowered by a sense of constituency in representing the broader voice. This approach quickly had some impact upon the prioritisation of initiatives that were already under consideration, and led to the development of new services in some districts. Most importantly, it provided a formal record of users' views and a valuable point of reference for evaluating progress.

This project showed how it was possible to increase contact amongst isolated service users and promote their voice. It demonstrated that there was a gulf between what professionals think they are saying and doing and users' perceptions of their efforts. Overall, this approach proved relatively inexpensive, costing only £2,500 for room hire, travel costs, crèches and refreshments, although this did not include the development worker's salary and on-costs. While some of the recommendations for developing services had substantial cost implications, many were relatively inexpensive to implement because they involved changes in attitudes, better information, or the sort of changes in working practices which do not intrinsically require additional funding. It is significant that social isolation and a consequent lack of support, together with public attitudes to mental health, were dominant themes that ran through much of the discussion. This project allowed sufficient time for the planning of the events, and most important, for training the users who acted as facilitators. Like the review of user participation reported by Lindow earlier, this project showed that success is unlikely, unless there is adequate preparation and support for those users who take on the crucial roles of advocates and facilitators. Payment for their time not only avoids potential exploitation of their goodwill and commitment, but sends an important message to them, and to other people, about the value of their contribution.

Morris (1994), in a study for the Social Services Policy Forum suggested that many of the features associated with self-help and user-controlled services, such as a greater willingness to listen and respond to people's needs and protests, greater participation and input into the development of services, a commitment to social justice, and a rejection of pathological models of problems, can be transferred to statutory and larger voluntary organisations. While this study did not focus upon rural areas, some of the features that she identified may be usefully applied to a rural context. Although the potential of some of these features arises from what might be described as being coincidences of perspective or points of potential agreement, as for example, when a social model of disability is a shared perspective, other features have a particular resonance for those seeking to develop services in rural areas. The promotion of a sense of common interest and common purpose may be more readily established where there are already some regional or area-based aspects of identity which can help override the basic division between those who provide and those who need services. More responsive and flexible services may be easier to establish when the numbers of potential clients is small and there is little in the way of existing service to predetermine what users should receive. Despite difficulties in transport and the absence of well-organised user groups in rural areas, user involvement may also be easier to develop when numbers are smaller.

User involvement clearly carries risk for service providers, in that it may well reveal the inadequacies of existing policies, practices and funding, and leave them vulnerable to criticism, but there is little to be gained by being defensive about such deficiencies. Furthermore, the implicit assumption that user involvement will inevitably be negative is mistaken and tends to indicate a rather defensive approach from the outset. In reality, service users are often very balanced in making their judgements, and perhaps if anything in rural areas, are a little too reticent to speak up. When users of community care services in Dorset were asked their views, they seem typical in that they strove for balance and generally were:

> *. . . understanding about the difficulties and accepted the inconvenience imposed by the need to travel long distances, or the fact that services were delivered at times not of their choosing. However, this did not deter them from expressing the view that they would like services to be more flexible.*
>
> (Social Services Inspectorate, 1998a, p30)

Involvement also carries risks for those users who participate, especially if it is used superficially 'to validate decisions that would have been made anyway' (Lucas, 1992, p14). It can be exploitative without proper support, training, and remuneration or recompense. One question that often arises is about the representativeness of the views expressed by user/participants. How can we be sure that these views are held more widely? The answer, of course, is that we cannot be certain, but we should not let this obscure the fact that efforts to engage with users are likely to reveal much more detailed information about preferences and problems than would otherwise be available to those who plan and provide services.

Worker perspectives and innovations

Over the last twenty years, social workers as a professional group have been confronted with considerable evidence of the inadequacies and the risks of their practice. Various scandals and numerous inquiries have demonstrated to the public at large and to the profession itself that it should be wary of making excessive claims as to what it is able to achieve. One consequence of this is that the profession as a whole has perhaps not been confident about its role in influencing policy. Arguably, the tendency has been to focus more upon technical matters and less upon broader issues of policy and practice. As a consequence, and for various reasons, British social workers have perhaps been somewhat reticent to claim expertise or to act as advocates for the development of broader policies (Aldridge, 1996). However, over the last ten years, the developing perspectives on anti-discriminatory and anti-oppressive practice have inculcated a more widespread awareness of how social work practice is located within the broader context of an unjust society, and helped workers to realise that their commitment to core values requires not simply that they avoid doing certain things, but that they actively engage to change circumstances where this is relevant and appropriate to their role. Even the Central Council for Education and Training in Social Work (CCETSW) acknowledged this broader responsibility within its requirements for qualifying training. Thus, the formal knowledge and the formal requirements that underpin qualifying training have begun to establish a more general expectation that social workers take an active part in policy formation and development.

While some workers have undoubtedly always subscribed to this view, many, and especially those working in local government, have tended to adopt a more passive view of their role and this vision of workers as rather passive apparatchiks has been reinforced by the dogmas of the managerialism which have been predominant in British public services over the past two decades. Nonetheless, these narrow views of social work are being challenged and especially, some of the more pessimistic portrayals of the future of social work (Pugh, 1997; Pugh and Gould, 2000). For example, the introduction of professional registers and the stronger framework of regulation, in which social workers are required to operate in accordance with practice guidance and codes of conduct, will lead to changes in the relationship between social workers as employees and their employers. The codification and regulation of their work will impose higher expectations about how they conduct their work and what level of responsibility they may be expected to take in regard to the adequacy of the services they provide. What may well follow from this is a realisation that they cannot sustain their professional role simply by acquiescing with the decisions of their employing agencies. Consequently, there is an opportunity for social work to develop a more optimistic picture of its own capacities, and prime among these is a greater engagement with policy making processes.

Opportunities for workers to engage in policy and service development in rural areas are mixed. While local policy making may be bedevilled by 'the big fish in a small pond' syndrome of individuals who seem to exercise a disproportionate level of influence on local affairs, paradoxically, there can be greater opportunities for workers to exercise some influence, because of:

- the lack of central government direction in regard to rurality
- the fact that party politics is often less polarised
- personal credibility is often a more valuable currency in smaller communities

Consequently, in rural areas where the political 'space' exists, workers who have ideas and who are well-known and respected in their personal and professional lives can often have far more influence upon the development of policy and services than their counterparts in urban settings. This can be used in a relatively unconscious manner, as when workers simply make decisions about how they will operate and with whom they will co-operate solely upon the basis of individual relationships (Martinez-Brawley, 1991). Alternatively, there may be an explicit recognition of their own credibility and consequent degree of autonomy which experienced and well-established workers can use to promote change. Many innovations in rural practice arise from the efforts of particular individuals who are able to initiate ideas and galvanise local support for them, and workers who seek change should always consider whether such opportunities exist. Martinez-Brawley (1991), notes that younger social workers in rural settings may feel more vulnerable and be less likely to challenge or contribute to the political debates about services. Indeed, there are other concomitant risks associated with developments which stem from individual initiatives. The first is that if the project becomes associated solely with one person it remains vulnerable if for any reason they are unable to carry on with the work. The second is that given the time it takes to get new developments going, innovations which do not mobilise a wider base of support are unlikely to succeed, because there may be resistance to any development, however inspired or well-meant, which could be perceived as being 'imposed' from without. There is much valuable advice in the literature on community development about avoiding such pitfalls, and Francis and Henderson give examples of successful initiation (1992), while Cox et al. (1987), provide a useful review of strategies for community organisation.

Joint Working: Inter-agency and Multi-agency Work

The terms inter-agency and multi-agency can be defined in rather different ways, but are often used loosely and interchangeably to refer to any efforts in which a number of organisations, statutory or independent, attempt to develop a common response to identifying, exploring and meeting needs. In this discussion, the term multi-agency is used to signify the fact of co-operation by two or more agencies aimed at some broader purpose external to them, and the term inter-agency is only used to indicate actions or communications between them, while the term joint working is preferred as a general descriptor which avoids potential confusions. Although a full discussion of the finer distinctions and the merits of inter-agency and multi-agency work is beyond the scope of this book, it is important to recognise that the ubiquity of these terms is a marker of their currently fashionable status and that it might be prudent to develop a critical appreciation of the potential advantages and disadvantages of joint working.

The widespread acceptance of the desirability of multi-agency approaches in all area of practice owes much to the failings revealed by official inquiries into numerous child protection cases, where children's safety has been compromised by inadequate co-operation and communication between agencies. Consequently, government documents such as the *Working To-gether* guidance (1991, 1999), have emphasised the shared responsibility of agencies and stressed the need for an integrated approach to child protection. Similarly, the various community care initiatives that preceded the National Health Services and Community Care Act 1990 and the subsequent difficulties and shortcomings in its implementation, have created a widespread acceptance of the need for joint working and co-operation in other areas of practice. Nevertheless, research into joint working has revealed a number of difficulties, and Hague (1999), in a review of multi-agency initiatives summarises some of the more general problems. Specifically:

- The tendency of some agencies to 'defend their own turf'.
- Potential confusion about roles and responsibilities which can arise from lack of clarity.
- A tendency to marginalise equality issues such as gender and ethnicity.
- When multi-agency initiatives are used as a cynical face-saving strategy to avoid confronting shortages of resources.
- The consumption and wastage of scarce resources, especially of smaller agencies, in unproductive discussion.
- The futility of attempts to co-ordinate systems that are already inadequate or disorganised.
- The difficulties in resolving differences of power, resources and philosophy between agencies.
- A tendency for larger agencies to take over the work and marginalise the smaller agencies, sometimes even when they were the original initiators of the project.
- Alternatively, when larger agencies leave too much of the work to smaller ones.
- The tendency to marginalise service users and prospective clients.

These difficulties are not intrinsic or inevitable aspects of joint working, and it is sensible to consider them as potential risks which, with foresight, commitment, clear aims and strategy, can be avoided or mitigated. Some of the problems stem from conflicting imperatives within different legislation which can result in rather different agency perceptions of roles and responsibilities in particular situations. For example, while the Children Act 1989 requires social services to seek the opinion of a young person before making any decisions as to their welfare, education law leaves parents with sole rights (Eaton, 1995). In some instances, agencies may have developed different criteria for intervention, while in others, participants may tend to see conflict as a result of different personalities. This tendency to personalise or pathologise is also evident when difficulties are interpreted as signs of problems within an agency, rather than as structural problems arising from the interaction of bureaucratic systems (Eaton, 1995). Inter-agency communication has been an issue since the Monkton Report in 1945, which revealed the shortcomings in communication surrounding the death of Dennis O'Neill, and despite considerable reinforcement of this aspect of multi-agency work, it continues to be problematic. In some instances, agencies have failed to check whether their onward referrals to other agencies have been responded to, while in others, they have relied upon the service user to act as the medium of communication between them. Despite the rhetoric of multi-agency work, agencies may still neglect their professional responsibility to communicate effectively with each other (Eaton, 1995).

Nevertheless, despite the pitfalls of multi-agency work it is obviously a necessary feature of social service provision. For example, when needs do not fall neatly into pre-existing areas of agency responsibility, and where co-ordination is essential to respond adequately to the particularities of people's situations. Eaton, in a study of services to young people with special needs and in difficulty, found that their problems were often 'defined according to how they fit into the work of agencies rather than by an analysis of what they need; they therefore tend to be seen either as on the margin, or outside of, any one particular service' (1995, p1). The risk of potential clients 'falling between' agencies has probably increased since the reorganisation of the National Health Service and local government has reduced the 'fit' between the areas which they respectively serve. One consequence is that some health authorities who previously worked with one or two local authorities now have to work with as many as six bodies. Not only does this take much longer to do, but it has shifted the balance of power in the multi-agency relationship, with the larger health authorities tending to be more dominant in joint planning (Craig and Manthorpe, 1999).

Despite the risk of joint-working being used a 'face saving' initiative when resources are scarce, it is a legitimate response to scarcity providing that the shortage is explicitly acknowledged as one of the stimuli to the project. In fact, in rural areas where higher service delivery costs are often unavoidable, in the medium term at least, it remains the most practical way of improving user access and choice. Apart from the obvious advantages arising from better co-ordination of activities, Hague (1999), identifies several other potential advantages of joint working, especially when it occurs between statutory and voluntary organisations, where it can help:

- raise awareness of problems and issues within statutory bodies
- provide better channels of communications between potential users and providers
- organisations to develop their own policy and practice guidance
- develop better information about existing resources and provision

As noted earlier, there are several obvious reasons why agencies may wish and may need to work together, but in practice, partnership on any but the smallest and most local of projects is often hard work, and partnership between statutory and independent agencies is often accompanied by rather different perspectives upon the 'problem'. Commitment to some common goal is essential, and agencies should clarify from the outset what the rationale or motivation for their partnership might be, as this helps shape realistic expectations about what they may be able to achieve together. Joint working may be stimulated by:

- Statutory requirement or policy directive from central government.
- Economic necessity, where no single agency can afford to fund a project alone.
- A common commitment to a project for which no agency alone bears sole responsibility.
- The need to broaden the base of support by enlisting other people and other agencies to help carry an existing initiative forward, or to extend its field of operation.
- The desire to seek acceptance and to legitimate an initiative that might otherwise be controversial or be resisted by a particular community or potential service users.
- A common recognition that a multi-agency approach is a necessity.
- The wish to avoid being seen as the agency with sole responsibility.

This is not an exhaustive list of motivations, but it helps focus upon the primary reasons why a partnership is being mooted in the first place. However, even when motivations may seem a little cynical or half-hearted, the process of actually working together can change the perspectives of participants and sometimes lead to a more positive commitment to the enterprise. However, if change is not forthcoming, then small organisations may need to consider whether to commit any further time and resources to projects that appear to be marking time and where there is little sign of positive commitment to action (Hague, 1999).

The use of partnerships to enlist local support and to avoid potential resistance is an important feature of rural initiatives, because there is often resistance to agencies coming in from outside and imposing their 'solutions'. This resistance is frequently interpreted as political conservatism, and indeed in some instances it may be so, but often the reasons for it are structural. Small communities may engender solidarity by avoiding overt dissent and by often seeking to establish the appearance of consensus, especially on contentious issues. Such, resistance may have complex foundations. Sometimes it may be focused upon the specifics of a proposal which are felt to be inappropriate or unnecessary, and sometimes it may arise from the social dynamics of a community in rural districts. For example, Dhalech, in reporting the development of anti-racist initiatives in south-west England, notes that:

> *Some black agencies came into the area wanting to undertake development work but they typically lacked an understanding of rural issues . . . An officer from a national agency offered support for developing a telephone help line modelled on a London borough. The several meetings between the officer and representatives of local Black agencies proved to be remarkably unconstructive because there was no recognition of rural issues. As soon as the local agencies started discussing the idea between themselves an immediate consensus was reached and the ideas were developed.*

> (Dhalech, 1999, p29)

This illustrates a very important point and one well documented within the literature on community development work, which is that success is most likely when a community or a group takes on board the need for change itself and determines its own direction, its priorities, and commits itself to the development and implementation of the proposal (Francis and Henderson, 1992). Strangely, while most social workers seem to appreciate, almost instinctively, the premise in one-to-one work that you should 'start from where the client is', some fail to recognise the importance of applying this to the initiation of projects in the wider community. Thus, they sometimes begin with a naive assumption that 'good ideas' are self-evidently so, and will in themselves elicit wider support. In contrast, community workers are more likely to appreciate that 'ownership' may be everything in terms of enhancing the success of a project.

All service providers may have much to gain from partnerships with development bodies and academic institutions. For example, Action with Rural Communities in England (ACRE), developed a poverty mapping project in Dorset in partnership with the county council and Oxford University. Such mixed partnerships often facilitate access to sources of funding, such as charitable organisations and research bodies, which would not otherwise be available to one or other of the partners. One difficulty that faces voluntary organisations is that because many funding initiatives are short term they often create pressure to bid quickly for funds, and if successful, to spend money within a relatively short period of time. This can lead to inappropriate attempts to apply models of service delivery which have been developed in an urban context into a rural one, and so fail to take sufficient account of differences in geography, demography and attitudes to services (Gibson et al., 1995). Mason and Taylor, in a report for the Gulbenkian Foundation, provided sound advice about the development and funding of projects, and laid particular emphasis upon the need to allow enough time for project proposals to be developed properly, 'Projects in rural areas take much longer than their urban counterparts to get started and established. A much longer lead-in time is required, so that three years may not be enough' (1990, p38). They also suggest that the requirement to be innovatory, which is often a criterion of funding, should not be interpreted in such a way as to exclude the development of existing ideas into new areas.

The importance of adequate 'lead-in' time was reinforced in a more recent study of the development of community based partnership for development in rural areas by Edwards et al., which found that:

> *The lead-in time for preparing bids to programmes, and partnership initiation, is frequently too short to enable appropriate structures and sustainable relationships to be constructed ... This 'establishment phase' is particularly crucial as partnerships tend to be very stable once set up.*
>
> (1999, p2)

Eaton's study also showed that there were 'few mechanisms for the joint exploration of issues arising from individual cases or for feeding this into strategic planning and preventative work (1995, p1). Midgley et al., in a small study of user involvement and multi-agency working to improve housing for older people found that 'multi-agency policy making ... (was) patchy at best, and at worst is virtually non-existent' (1997, p1), although they found widespread agreement among users, carers, campaigners and professionals about what would be the desirable properties of a good housing system. Some of these desirable characteristics relate solely to housing, but there were five aspects that could be generalised to any form of multi-agency work. Specifically, that:

- a wide diversity of agencies should co-ordinate their activities
- a single, participative assessment should generate multiple options from a variety of agencies

- user choice should be maximised
- user involvement should be promoted
- qualitative information should be systematically used in planning

(1997, p3)

The model of multi-agency working that was developed in this study had four main elements. First, the work of the different agencies was linked by a co-ordinator who chaired multi-agency meetings, and also helped people to make connections and referrals. Second, a joint assessment scheme was developed in which a single assessment could be used to access services from different agencies. This used cross-agency training to develop the skills of assessment officers. Third, qualitative information about needs and services was collected by outreach workers who reported the accounts of service users, which together with information about agency resources, problems and opportunities, was fed into a policy making multi-agency planning board. Fourth, this planning board had a shadow board made up of user-representatives who had access to all the same information.

While there may be reservations about the effectiveness of this parallel body and the imbalance of power, and indeed, other alternative structures may work better in different circumstances, the point is that this model does offer a way of developing strategic responses from individual experiences and institutionalises feedback to planning bodies. In fact, this model meets many of the points that Eaton (1995), believes characterise good multi-agency work, for it:

- Requires formal commitment and support from senior management and from political to practitioner level.
- Creates a forum for discussion of policies, practices, and the development of strategic planning.
- Develops common working practices on crucial aspects of service provision and procedures.
- Encourages the development of common ownership of problems and responses.
- Has mechanisms for sharing information, particularly that which requires some degree of confidentiality.
- Has some joint training to establish common procedures and understanding of roles and responsibilities.
- Encourages joint monitoring and evaluation of services in regard to formal aims and users' needs and perceptions.

A prime objective of most local Community Care Plans is to further develop integration between primary health care services, that is, general practitioners, district nursing and health centres, and social care and social services for adults. One way of doing this has been to link social workers with particular general practices. For example, in Wiltshire over half of GP surgeries and team practices had a link worker, this was a jointly funded care manager post, and many other practices had a named social services person who provided regular advice sessions, or with whom they had regular discussions about services (SSI, 1998b). Some areas of service require joint commissioning, particularly when people's problems do not fall exclusively within the realm of one service, as where people with learning disabilities or frail elderly people also have mental health problems.

Working with Voluntary Organisations

Edwards et al. (1999), identified four crucial features in developing partnerships between statutory agencies and voluntary organisations:

- Time, resources and training for community involvement. Often, potential partners feel that they need more time to consult with their communities before the final plans are consolidated, and some feel unprepared and disadvantaged because they feel unable to contribute at the same level as other partners. Start-up money can help small voluntary organisations participate more effectively in these early stages before funding comes on-stream.
- Recognition of different partners' cultures. Partnership working requires particular skills, and ways or modes of working which may be unfamiliar to some potential partners, who may find the apparently slow pace of progress and the continuing need for accountability frustrating.
- Time and resources to build trust. 'Prejudices between partners can create obstacles to effective co-operation until the expertise of each partner is proved' (1999a, p3). Good administration and communications are essential to the creation of confidence in a project.
- Stable programmes of adequate duration. The very nature of limited life funding for many programmes tends to compromise the time available for proving the stability of projects to partners and other participants, so they need to be realistic in their expectations of what may be achievable within certain time frames. Pre-existing experience of partnerships often contributes greatly to success in funding applications and in the continuance of innovatory projects beyond their initial funding period.

The lead agencies, either because they are the funding agency or because they have existing responsibilities and experience, have a major role in facilitating and sometimes, in selecting partners. The question of which organisations and people to engage with in the first place will usually set the 'terms' for the discussions that will subsequently occur, so the question of just who is engaged with is very important. In urban areas there may well be some easily identifiable organisations with a clear remit which matches the aim of a particular project, and this is frequently the case with user-groups for people with particular forms of disability. However, in rural areas there may be no obvious organisations other than those which serve more general purposes, such as parish councils, religious organisations, women's institutes, community councils and other associations. While these can be important sources of information and support, they should not preclude direct attempts to get closer to potential users. Local meetings, surveys, community radio and the press will often provide a platform from which to consult other people about local needs and to publicise proposed initiatives.

The review undertaken by Hague (1999), has already been used to reveal some of the difficulties faced by voluntary organisations in joint working with the statutory sector, but it also indicated some of the difficulties and dilemmas for the individuals involved. For volunteers and workers who are committed activists it can be especially frustrating when statutory organisations begin to 'take over' projects, and appear to marginalise them and the users of their services. One interviewee, talking about joint working on a 'domestic violence' project, reported that:

> *In the forum, there are problems about power—the already powerful groups trying to take control—paralleling the process of abuse—the watchword is 'co-operation' not 'competition'. There is a parallel process in the committee in terms of working with domestic violence—a lot of power play between agencies mirroring what often happens in a relationship.*

> (Hague, 1999, p102)

Larger organisations need to develop a more sophisticated understanding of power and how it is perceived by small voluntary organisations such as women's aid groups and disability activists, who have developed a political analysis of their own situation in society. For such groups and individuals, who understand the myriad ways in which the personal is indeed political, will be especially attuned to the nuances of interpersonal and organisational power in their dealings with more powerful agencies and individuals.

Acquiring and maintaining satisfactory levels of funding is a perennial problem for voluntary organisations, especially since the shift towards community care has led to increasing demand for the service provided by some organisations. A long term study of 16 voluntary organisations in

London and Sheffield undertaken by Alcock et al. (1999b), found that the annual round of 'panic fundraising' made it 'chronically difficult to plan strategically' (1999a, p1). Although there are different patterns of funding, many voluntary bodies rely heavily upon government agencies for funding, and most devoted a considerable amount of effort to maintaining these links. Interestingly, this study found that there was no 'preferred' pattern of funding, for there were advantages and disadvantages associated with both single and multiple funding sources:

Reliance on one major funder created vulnerability to shifting funding priorities, for example, and a more diverse funding base gave organisations a stronger position from which to cope with such shifts. However, having a range of funders in support also meant workers and volunteers expending much time and energy dealing with them all and managing different demands and operational time scales.

(Alcock et al., 1999a, p3)

This study produced some sound advice for funders as well as for voluntary organisations themselves. For funders, they suggested that:

- Some funding for core functions can help voluntary organisations become more sustainable, especially when so many are highly dependent upon one key person to drive their day to day work.
- Clarity about the 'grand goals' is helpful to voluntary organisations who have to decipher and respond to rather fuzzy terminology, for example, the aim of 'capacity building' created confusion for many organisations.
- Better liaison and greater collaboration between different funding bodies would help voluntary organisations better organise and conserve their resources in regard to bidding for funding, and by creating more uniform procedures for the evaluation and monitoring of projects.
- There is a need for support to encourage voluntary organisations to take a more strategic approach to medium and long term planning. For example, recurrent grants can avoid the annual resource-consuming round of 'grant chasing'.
- They need to review the use of consultants to help voluntary organisations to develop complex funding bids.

For voluntary organisations, the recommendations parallel the advice to funders. The study suggested that they should use local networks for support, especially if they can assist with core functions, avoid over-dependence upon a single 'key' person, develop medium and longer term strategic plans, make sure that their management or steering committees met the expectations of funders, and develop collaborative funding bids based upon multiple sources of funding.

Supporting the Workforce

The general issue of how to train and support workers in the personal social services is one that is extensively addressed elsewhere (Fineman, 1985; Hawkins and Shohet, 1989; Kadushin, 1976; Morrison, 1993; Yelloly and Henkel, 1995), and it is not the aim of this short section to reproduce the sound guidance offered by others, but instead, to point up what for some workers is the dominant characteristic of social work in a rural context, namely, isolation. Rural workers are often relatively isolated and unsupported in their work and this can stem from a basic lack of social support and encouragement, a lack of proper supervision, a lack of interaction with an informed professional peer group, as well as the absence of any obvious back-up to provide cover or workload relief.

For many rural workers, it is their family and friends who provide the social support that helps them keep going, but there are some real problems for professionally isolated individual workers, especially those on limited life projects who may not be well integrated into the community they serve. While membership of professional bodies and contact with workers in other schemes may be valuable sources of advice and support, they do not tackle the most fundamental problem which is the lack of effective supervision, which can be an issue for both paid and unpaid workers. Indeed, well prepared and trained volunteers are often crucial to the success of rural initiatives, but they do not always realise themselves how important their contribution is (Gibson et al., 1995), or what their supervision needs might be. Consequently, there is a need to make sure that volunteers receive supervision to support them and help maintain their morale and commitment. They also need feedback on their performance so that they have opportunities to amend and develop it. When individual volunteers are working within organised schemes of care and support, some means of oversight is also required to monitor the quality of the service provided and resolve any difficulties that occur. The Anglican Church has provided some useful elementary advice on organising rural care and is very clear about the need for supervision, which it acknowledges 'may sound threatening to a volunteer, but it is essential to have some system for monitoring the service so that any problems involving either the client or volunteer are easily resolved as part of a recognised routine' (Savigear, 1996, p9).

For workers who live in the area in which they work, the close contact with the local community can be a cause of stress, especially when their formal duties do not always meet with local approval. In the absence of good supervision, workers can feel very exposed and often do not have the informal support of the larger work group of colleagues that is usually evident in urban areas. It is vital that managers provide adequate support for their workers, and where they are employed by small voluntary bodies, that the trustees or managers consider how they can ensure that workers have opportunities to:

- share concerns and off load their anxieties appropriately
- meet with other people engaged in similar work
- develop their knowledge and skills
- explain and justify their actions
- review and reflect upon their practice
- check the appropriateness of their proposed actions
- get feedback upon their performance

It is especially important that those who work largely alone, without the supportive presence and formal structures usually found in larger agencies, feel that they are not the sole proselytisers or defenders of the service. When misunderstandings and conflicts develop in small communities, workers need to feel that they have support, and there is an important role for their managers who may have to consider how to help the local community understand what has happened, and help it to appreciate some of the reasons why the service has responded as it has. This can raise difficult questions about confidentiality, but when such discord occurs, it is often surprising to find out how much is already widely known within a small community. Although indirectness is a common feature of communication in rural areas (see Part 3), people may still have high expectations about the level of knowledge they will eventually expect to receive. Skilled managers and workers will learn when and how to reveal information which does not compromise any commitments to confidentiality, but nonetheless, allows local networks to better understand what has been happening. Sometimes, in the absence of management support, the worker's own local contacts may informally undertake this vital explanatory role.

Evaluating Services

Policy and practice development needs to be informed by feedback about existing services, but few departments have any coherent policy on evaluation, and even fewer have a systemic approach to gathering such information and using it. This section is not a review of the methodological issues, for there is an extensive literature on this aspect of evaluation, instead it focuses upon of the frame of reference and the criteria that are used in assessing the adequacy of rural services. There are two broad approaches that can be taken in evaluating rural services. The first is to construct a theoretical model which provides the major dimensions for investigation and comparison. This is the approach developed by Martinez-Brawley (1982, 1986, 1991), who contends that rural services should be organised around, and analysed in terms of, three main concepts, generalism, localism, and community orientation, thus:

> *Generalism or generalist services refers not only to the entry level at which the client gains access to the social services (in Britain, for example, the single door model of the county social service department), but also to the orientation of the worker in providing help. Localism or locality specific services refers to the degree of individualization of the services given the unique linguistic, cultural and infrastructural characteristics of the area to which they are being provided ... (it) can also refer to the level of government at which services are administered, whether close to the client or by a remote and bureaucratic structure ... community-oriented services refer to the degree to which they incorporate and support natural systems, traditional structures, etc. It also refers to the degree to which social workers help energize communities to partake in their own care ...*
>
> (Martinez-Brawley, 1991, p271)

Martinez-Brawley presents these three concepts not simply as dimensions for analytical comparison but also as desirable principles which she sees as self-evidently 'essential in the provision of social services to the rural areas of most countries in the western world (1991, p270). While we may accept the desirability of these concepts as general organising principles, and indeed as we have seen elsewhere in this book, there may be many good reasons to do so, it is possible to use these concepts for the purposes of evaluation in a less prescriptive manner. Of course, evaluation should seek to measure what is provided against some notional standards, otherwise it can be a rather pointless exercise, but given that our knowledge of what works best in rural work is limited, it might be a mistake to assume the desirability of these concepts completely. Furthermore, it is possible to conceive of circumstances in which generalisation and localisation are undesirable elements within service provision, as for example, when seeking to enhance access to services for sexually transmitted diseases, or when working with the perpetrators of child abuse. Indeed community-orientation may be quite problematic when local attitudes are intolerant or hostile to those whom we seek to help. Nevertheless, despite these reservations and the lack of wider usage, this model does have some potential for evaluation, and especially for comparative evaluation in the way in which Martinez-Brawley has used it to examine services in different countries.

The second approach is more clearly prescriptive and is currently being developed by the Department of Health, their counterparts in Northern Ireland, Scotland and Wales, and the Social Services Inspectorates. Previously, these bodies have not provided much guidance in regard to the evaluation of rural services, but increasingly, through various initiatives and policies, such as evidence-based practice and *Best Value*, they are promoting an approach to evaluation that aims to improve the transparency and accountability of social services departments in their work, by requiring them to provide definite statements of targets and achievements. For example, the inspections into community care services in the countryside undertaken in 1998/9 have resulted in a statement of standards against which rural services will be judged. The five standards against which services will be evaluated are:

- Responsiveness—service users in rural communities, and their carers, receive services which are responsive to their needs.
- Accessibility—service users and their carers receive services which are accessible within their local communities and, where this is impractical, alternatives are negotiated with them.
- Information and communication—service users in rural communities, and their carers are well informed about community care services.
- Equal opportunities—service users and carers are to be treated fairly and with respect for their particular lifestyles. Policies should encompass the particular equal opportunity needs of people who live in rural communities.
- Management arrangements—the SSD has management arrangements which develop and deliver best value services which are responsive to the needs of its rural population.

(Social Services Inspectorate, 1999, pp57–61)

Under each standard is a list of more specific criteria which they used to devise a checklist of questions for their inspections, and which local authorities can use themselves to review their services, and these could also be adapted by voluntary organisations for their own purposes. These questions include:

- Have people who live in rural areas been involved in developing services appropriate to their needs?
- Do staff consult service users about how, and from whom, they would prefer to receive services, for example, from local people or from strangers?
- Do the services provided support informal care arrangements?

- Do budgetary arrangements operate sufficiently flexibly to allow for local commissioning where this is appropriate to meet local needs?
- Are you confident that services are provided equitably and appropriately across the LA? How do you know?

(Social Services Inspectorate, 1999, pp14–18)

In their review, the Inspectorate also conducted a postal survey of service users, and from the 475 responses, a return rate of 60 per cent, found that 79 per cent were satisfied with the services they had received and 91 per cent thought the departments' staff were helpful. The main sources of respondents' dissatisfaction arose from the distance they had to travel to obtain some services and from the lack of choice in terms of the range of services. While the overall levels of satisfaction appear encouraging, we should be wary of reading too much into these responses. This survey only addressed existing users and did not access those who received no help. Furthermore, the question of low expectations from service users is not addressed, yet there is evidence from other sources which suggest that this is a prevalent feature of rural dwellers' expectations of public services generally. It should be recognised that these are only the first stages in developing the evaluation and review of rural services and that it may be necessary to broaden the range of issues that are examined, but in the light of the general lack of evaluation of social services, this approach is potentially useful because it focuses attention upon the question of what constitutes a satisfactory service. From an anti-discriminatory perspective the main issue that remains unresolved is the extent to which service users are themselves able to participate in setting the agenda for evaluation, and whether they have any subsequent role in determining service priorities and provision?

Conclusion

We should not delude ourselves into thinking that the difficulties of providing suitable rural social services will be solved simply by the success of the persuasive case that can be made for a rural premium in funding services. Of course, this will make a significant difference, but the problems of higher costs arising from dispersed populations, small numbers, less support available from fewer voluntary organisations, and the obstacles of insufficient information about existing needs combined with potential users' resistance to seeking help, their lack of knowledge about what services might be available, and their generally lower expectations of services, means that statutory social services will never be able to respond satisfactorily to all of the potential needs that may exist. Diversity of provision is essential if consumers are to have some choice about where, and from whom, they may seek help. Consequently, statutory bodies must recognise their statutory obligations and should work in partnership with each other and with other independent sector agencies to research, plan, commission and provide services. It remains to be seen whether *Best Value* does result in more open government, more sharing of information across local authorities and better services. Scepticism about policy initiatives like *Best Value* is understandable, since it may be seen as yet another attempt to get local authorities to deliver improved services with little or no new money. Nevertheless, it also represents an attempt to change the organisational culture in terms of commissioning services. Most significantly, unlike Compulsory Competitive Tendering, it allows for the consideration of 'non-commercial' issues such as equal opportunities in regard to access to services, diversity of provision and consultation. This drive towards clarity of objectives and outcomes is epitomised in the words of Denise Platt, the Chief Inspector of Social Services, who said:

> *Successful social services ask people what they want and explain what they can expect. They learn what works and how to deliver it. They measure what they do, count what services cost and support their staff.*

(Audit Commission, 2000, p2)

Co-operation and partnership can provide opportunities for some economies of scale, and allow a more effective use of the available resources. This is evident in those initiatives which have developed multi-use facilities, joint funding, or have developed multi-disciplinary working methods, as well as those which have built upon the specialisation of skills such as counselling and advice-giving. Statutory bodies will need to develop a more sophisticated appreciation of the problems of independent service providers, especially in regard to voluntary organisations and their need to escape the vagaries of short term planning and funding cycles. Innovations that are well-grounded in local communities rather than being perceived as imposed from without, are much more likely to mobilise the support of significant people in the community, and so ensure the longer term viability of new services. But before this can happen, there is often a fundamental challenge facing those who seek to develop new services, which is to persuade others of the need for particular initiatives at the outset. The rural context may not necessarily be a more conservative context than its urban counterpart, but it may well be perceived by those who live there as a less diverse one. Consequently, an appreciation of particular problems and difficulties may be much harder to promote and establish, and it is clear from many rural projects that it does take much longer to create and develop new services.

While social workers in urban areas may often find themselves and their agencies responding to demands articulated by others, in rural areas workers may often have to take a much more proactive stance to promoting the voice of other people and, indeed, to promoting their own ideas within their agencies and communities. The personal and professional credibility that individuals can build up over many years of service in rural areas can represent a significant resource for mobilising change, and may well be one that creates a greater sense of obligation for individual workers than they might experience in urban areas.

While this section provides some pointers as to how services and policies can be developed, it cannot provide a simple matrix for achieving this. The experience derived from many rural initiatives is that they often depend upon the commitment of a particular individual to get them going in the first place, and many remain vulnerable to changes in personnel, worker exhaustion and burnout. Many initiatives struggle to establish any efficiency gains because of small size and rarely benefit from any division of labour, or economies of scale. This is where co-operation and partnership can really pay dividends in terms of existing services supporting new projects through assistance with administration, accountancy services, planning expertise, mentoring and other means of supporting the often isolated and overburdened project development worker. Furthermore, in many small scale projects, these resource constraints and the lack of 'social distance' between workers and clients lends greater impetus to the goal of user participation. The engagement of service users and their families in planning and developing services helps not only to ensure the appropriateness of what is being planned, but also provides a valuable social resource in terms of their participation legitimising the new development. The informality of small projects can enlist the support of users in helping to ensure the continued viability of the project in providing opportunities for direct help and support.

Part 3: Delivering Services in Rural Communities

Part 3 attempts to bring together the general information about rurality reviewed in Part 1 with the particular issues regarding the delivery of social services reviewed in Part 2. It begins by helping workers to understand how and why they need to become socially skilled in their work in rural areas, and then moves on to consider particular services, like those to children and families, community care, and services to travellers, and the response to specific issues, such as youth homelessness, racism, 'domestic violence', sexuality, drug misuse, and rural stress and suicide.

Becoming Socially Skilled in Rural Contexts

Arguably, there are few, if any, social skills that are unique to rural contexts, but there is little doubt that workers do need to use their skills in an informed way. That is, by considering the particular situations of individuals within the context of the more general knowledge that we have about rural contexts and by using this knowledge to shape the ways in which we communicate, negotiate, intervene, and evaluate our practice.

Professional stance, personal presentation and credibility

The lack of anonymity in rural life that has been noted elsewhere in this book, and which is further considered in the sections on confidentiality and personal safety, extends to both parties, to workers as well as to clients. Ellen Walsh, writing about rural mental health practice in the USA, observed that:

> ... clients who encounter their therapist at the cafe, the post office, and community gatherings are likely to be acutely sensitive to differences in personal style between these gatherings and the treatment session.
> (Walsh, 1989, p587)

Although the form of practice that she is describing is not one that many British workers engage in, her point is pertinent. The consequences of the worker's lack of anonymity can be far-reaching and can have implications for their sense of separation of home and work life, for personal safety, and most immediately, for the ways in which social workers comport themselves socially, and in their work. This aspect of rural practice is rarely noted within the scarce British literature on rural practice, and yet is almost always alluded to by rural social workers when they talk about their practice. Phrases like 'down to earth', and 'calling a spade a spade' are sometimes used to represent the apparent straightforwardness and robustness of approach that is believed to characterise rural behaviour, and certainly for many farmers, the close contact with the cycles of life and death in their animals can seem to be extended to their own lives. Indeed, at one large rural practice with several doctors, each with a very different personality, a colleague observed that most farmers seemed to prefer the most brusque and plain speaking of the doctors, who was widely perceived as 'giving it to them straight'. Conversely, incomers, especially those from urban areas, tended to prefer to be seen by other doctors from whom they expected a more measured and less direct approach. Similarly social workers who might be perceived as being overly voluble, 'above themselves', too 'flashy', and 'citified' may also experience difficulties in establishing effective relationships with their service users.

Ellen Walsh suggests that the 'emphasis upon self-sufficiency, personal responsibility, and self-determination in the rural community value system' (1987, p587) can enhance the chances of success in social work practice in the countryside. These qualities, where they exist, can result in clients having much more realistic and pragmatic expectations of social services, and can make them 'more likely to accept the concept of personal responsibility for change' (1987, p587). However, we should be wary of expecting such a simple picture of personal styles and especially wary of generalising from limited knowledge. The difficulty is that while there may well be certain traits of personal presentation that are more commonly observed, and perhaps expected from individuals, the likelihood is that judgements about the credibility of workers will rarely rest solely upon one or two aspects of their professional demeanour. Consequently, the judgements that clients make about workers cannot be assumed to rest upon an unvarying list of preferred characteristics, and nor should workers assume a parallel set of matching characteristics among service users. Ellen Walsh's point is that in smaller communities, people have more opportunities to observe each other's behaviour in a range of different situations and are well placed to observe discontinuities between the personal style and manner that is used within work and their behaviour and presentation elsewhere. Workers who may wish to maintain a professional 'distance', or even mistakenly some sense of 'mystique', will find it difficult to do this, because their 'otherness' and professional power may visibly be seen not to extend to other aspects of their particular rural context. Furthermore, some discontinuities may be read as evidence of insincerity or shallowness, and consequently perceived as indicating unreliability. The authenticity of the worker's professional persona can be checked more easily by rural service users living in smaller communities.

Placing

In Part 1 we noted how the social and physical geographies of an area encompassed mental maps which not only defined territory in terms of space but also in terms of who lived within it. The social aspects of such geographies also include an expectation that people identify themselves and 'place' each other, to a degree that is not commonly expected in urban areas. Many people in rural areas usually expect to have and to receive, directly or indirectly, more knowledge about the people with whom they interact than would most urban dwellers. Therefore, clients' judgements about workers can be based upon a much wider range of information that would typically be available in an urban area. For example, one worker who lived in a predominantly Welsh speaking district, but came from the south-east of England and still had her own strong local accent and spoke relatively little Welsh, was nevertheless well accepted in her community. This was helped by the fact that her children had grown up in the area, had attended Welsh medium schools and were well integrated into local life. But perhaps the most influential factor which promoted her acceptance was that before entering social work she had previously worked locally as a nurse. So, many people were aware of her good work, and had had the opportunity to form a judgement about her character and personality based upon direct contact, rather than upon any stereotypical perceptions of 'southerners' and incomers that they may have held.

All social workers are therefore likely to have to 'place' themselves in terms of where they live, whom they are related to, and so on. This obviously has implications for the way in which confidentiality is managed and maintained as well as for the ways in which we present ourselves in our professional role which were noted above. However, the main practical point of relevance here, is that workers need to be aware of how and why such placing is important and to be prepared to provide such information about themselves to prospective service users. This can be an unsettling experience for workers new to rural work and many seem to find it difficult initially to decide upon what is a suitable level of information. Their discomfort may stem from the loss of their usual assumption of anonymity outside of their work, as well as from a feeling that to give such information compromises the helping process and is perhaps self-indulgent and inappropriate. One worker who was providing a drop-in advice service for older people in a small rural town related how a previously unknown visitor, after establishing her original family name, stated; 'I knew your uncle, you know'. She was not sure exactly whom he was referring to, but replied, 'Oh, did you?' His subsequent response, 'Ah yes, he was a bugger, you know', left her in no doubt as to his allusion, meaning that he was a somewhat cussed person who had also been rather a tearaway in his youth. While the content of this exchange is hardly typical, the import of it certainly is. The subtext is that 'I know who you are and where you come from' and it also serves to remind the worker not to 'get above herself' or put on any unwanted professional airs and graces. In such ways, rural clients can use information about workers to offset the power imbalance that inevitably exists between helper and helped. It forms a powerful resource that can be manipulated and mobilised to establish one's position viz other people.

This aspect of rural life can operate negatively in terms of compromising one's own sense of privacy, but it can also be a very positive feature of practice in the countryside. One common consequence is that professional and personal credibility can be mutually reinforced as one's public and private social networks overlap, and furthermore, can be strengthened, as the word gets around about how one has discharged one's duties competently. The downside of course, is that the reverse may also occur. Rural social workers whose own teenage children are perceived as 'tearaways', or are out of control, will find little to comfort them in terms of any unquestioning acceptance of child rearing advice given to others. Information which may potentially discredit workers may not necessarily be based upon fact, but merely upon 'reputation'. This can be a difficult hurdle for social workers whose own lifestyle is perceived not to be 'normal', or is seen as marginal in some way. There is no easy solution to such difficulties, especially when the perception of difference is linked to negative ideas about the source or form of difference. For example, black, gay, or disabled practitioners and their colleagues and managers, will have to form some assessment of what perceptions other people may already have about them, without unwittingly legitimating the very forms of prejudice and discrimination that they are, at least nominally, committed to challenging. There is little reliable evidence as to what works best in such circumstances, but many workers whose working life has encompassed such difficulties have noted how these have diminished over time, and how their personal credibility has risen and become more generalised as other people have more experience and contact with them. The situation seems to be rather like the experience of difference reported in Part 1, that familiarity can in many cases lead to a contingent acceptance, and in some favourable circumstances, can lead to workers becoming significant individuals whose difference is acknowledged and widely accepted. One black worker asked about whether he thought racism dogged his practice, said that while it could do so, especially when he was in contact with incomers, most local people seemed to be quite protective of his potential vulnerability and would sometimes intercede on his behalf to see that he was treated fairly.

Practical tips:

- Be prepared to offer some information about oneself and one's family, but do not provide a potted biography, remember that the purpose of this interchange of information is not to show what a rounded or accomplished individual you are, but to establish your links with the wider community and to allow the would-be client to ascertain what risks accompany their engagement with your services.
- Look for potential points of location in terms of previous connections to particular localities, organisations, significant individuals and so on.
- Initially give implicit, and later, explicit reassurances about boundaries and confidentiality.
- Allow time for this 'getting to know' process to occur.

Communication

Practitioners should be aware that those aspects of communicative competence which enhance effective social work interaction in urban areas are just as valuably pursued in rural districts. The capacity to switch linguistic codes and to mix them appropriately, and to use an appropriate vocabulary, remain crucial aspects of communication (Pugh, 1996). While the characterisation of the typical country person as being a slow paced, taciturn and somewhat shy person has undoubtedly stereotypical elements to it, there is a grain of truth in the generalisation, in so far as country people will themselves often contrast the speedy pace of life in urban areas with the more measured tempo of social relations in rural areas. This self-conscious aspect of rural dwellers' perception of the pace of rural life can be an important factor in understanding and facilitating communication and requires workers to become more aware of their own capacity to mirror the pace of conversation and the pace of work.

There seem to be two reasons why more time is needed in rural interactions. The first is that there is a need to communicate more general information than might otherwise be required in an urban interaction where the worker and the client may not have any wider expectations about the extent to which they occupy a common 'social world'. The second is that the common communicative styles may typically entail more frequent and longer pauses between speakers and within utterances. Moreover, rural conversation, far from being stereotypically robust and direct, may often be more indirect and tentative. The value of indirectness in small rural communities is obvious, it is a valuable mitigating device for avoiding confrontation, and can ameliorate the potentially negative consequences of exercising power, expressing disagreement, or advancing criticism (Pugh, 1996). The words of the farmer who once said to me, 'you are a long time living with your mistakes around here', indicated his awareness that unguarded talk and conversational gaffes were more likely to be damaging in social networks where contact was infrequent. In rural areas, where people may be even more sensitive to the possibility of loosing services if they appear to criticise them, simply because there are fewer alternatives and because criticism may be taken more personally, it can be difficult to get feedback from users and their families. It is therefore crucial to use informal means of establishing peoples' views and this is largely dependent upon the quality of the communicative aspects of the relationships between workers and clients.

As we shall see in the following section, the risks of revealing potentially damaging or discrediting information about oneself are much more readily apparent in small communities where gossip can be a very powerful tool of inclusion or exclusion. Communicative competence requires workers to have a good cultural knowledge of the area in which they work. Indirectness can be an important means by which a client can establish whether a worker is attuned to their situation. For example, rather than explicitly state their problem, clients may often use a particular phrase or make an oblique reference to see whether the worker picks up its significance. In this way, they can 'test the water' to see how sensitively the worker reacts to their situation, without committing themselves to having to reveal information that an otherwise insensitive or unthinking person might misunderstand. This strategy, together with the often slower pace of conversation, means that workers might also need to respond with a similar indirectness, both to test their perception of what has been left unsaid, and also to show that they understand its significance. Typically this might be done by not responding immediately to the subtle cue, but by returning to it after a longer pause, or little later in the conversation. However, a worker who leaves it too long to signal her/his understanding can unsettle a client who may have assumed that the cue was not picked up. An acknowledgement that is delayed too long may transgress the expectation of 'selective forgetting' that is also required to be signalled if the participants are to meet each other without causing embarrassment in different circumstances in the future.

Privacy and Confidentiality

The potentially higher social visibility of the client and the worker within the smaller social networks and communities of the countryside which, as we noted earlier, requires workers to be authentic in the ways in which they present themselves in their work, also has implications for how issues of privacy and confidentiality are tackled. For these may be compromised in ways that do not seem immediately obvious to workers who are not familiar with rural life. For example, because many urban dwellers think of the countryside as an 'empty' space they assume that the absence of people and houses means that their actions are not being observed to the same degree as in cities and towns. In fact, the opposite is true. In areas where few people pass by and strangers are often readily apparent, there are often much higher levels of informal 'surveillance'. New visitors, unexplained changes to familiar routines, different times of coming and going, and new domestic arrangements may be the subject of observation and speculation.

A social work practice teacher reported how the experience of a student from an urban area who was on a rural placement with in mid-Wales, helped the student to appreciate how visible she was. Apparently, she had had some difficulty in finding the house she was visiting, and stopped to ask the way at another house a few miles away. The occupant politely gave her directions, and she continued on her way. By the time she had got to the house she wanted, the person she was hoping to see already knew that she was coming. Obviously, the person who had given her directions earlier had telephoned ahead to alert the household to her impending visit. This student learned a valuable lesson about how easy it was to unwittingly compromise a client's right to privacy by asking for directions when in an unfamiliar area. The visibility of both workers and clients can create real difficulties, when even an unfamiliar car passing 'up the lane' is an event worthy of notice. Clearly, social workers need to understand how rural networks operate in order to appreciate the possible reactions to their own behaviour and presence, otherwise confidentiality and privacy may easily be compromised by a thoughtless approach to home visiting and practice more generally. Even the safety of a woman who is attempting to escape a violent partner may be compromised by any attempt to use a local taxi or bus service, but this lack of confidentiality can extend even to the mail that people receive. In areas where the postman or postwoman knows many people and are known to many, then the mere receipt of a letter with an official envelope or postmark may be noted and commented upon. Nevertheless, as we noted in Part 2, there is often a higher expectation within a small community that people will eventually discover what has been happening. In fact, many clients may share these expectations and will themselves be acutely conscious of how things may be perceived. Thus, they will sometimes indicate that they are willing to have some information shared or 'released' on to the local networks of gossip and communication, and indeed, may do this without the assistance of the worker. The point is that workers need to be very sensitive to these currents of communication and learn how to cope with them, and even perhaps to manipulate them where they are clear that it is both in the best interest of their client, and does not compromise their professional position.

Practical tips:

- Written communications should be enclosed in plain envelopes, and in situations where confidentiality may be a particular cause for concern, agencies should use ordinary stamps or franking that does not identify the sender.
- When making telephone calls to clients who may wish to keep their involvement with social services private even within their own household, workers should consider using the facility to withhold their number so that it is not available for caller display or 1471 recall. In many larger switchboard systems this happens anyway, but there are some circumstances when this would not be appropriate, for example, in making a call to anyone who may have good reason to fear the identity of their callers.
- While there may be travel difficulties facing clients in more remote areas, workers should not assume that a home visit will be preferred. In situations where workers have the option to offer a choice of venue, this should be routinely offered. Similarly, any other arrangements for contact, by telephone or letter, should also be checked as to their suitability with the client at some point during the first contact.
- Clients should routinely be offered the opportunity to switch to another worker if pre-existing knowledge, or more recently discovered social connections, seem likely to impair their confidence in the confidentiality or suitability of their contact with a particular worker.
- Workers should try to ascertain what level of confidentiality is appropriate and is desired by a client in a situation.
- Outreach work can often be usefully situated in 'neutral' premises which do not identify the visitor's intentions to other people who may be passing-by.

Workers should not assume that a person's sexuality is necessarily an issue when working with homosexual men and women, but they should be aware of how it might be relevant especially for those who are not 'out' in the community. For example, a gay partner whose lover has died, and who has difficulty in expressing their grief when other family members are unaware of the nature of their relationship in an urban area, is likely to face even greater problems in acknowledging it within what they perceive to be an intolerant, or unsophisticated rural community. In such circumstances, the worker may become, in Goffman's words, one of the 'wise', a person trusted with privileged information. Despite this, the client may always feel vulnerable to the risks of disclosure or breach of confidentiality. Consequently, as noted in the earlier section on communication, they may 'test the water' by indirect references to what they see as risky information, to see whether the worker picks up the significance of the cue, and to help them ascertain the worker's sensitivity to their concerns.

Personal Safety

The violence and aggression that social workers face has increasingly become a source of concern over the past fifteen years (Department of Health, 1997; Norris, 1990), and among the expanding literature of developing safer practice, the training pack developed by More (1997), provides a valuable resource, and Bibby's book is very comprehensive (1994). Many of the factors that contribute to risk in rural work are the same as those prevailing in urban areas, and though rural workers are much less exposed to violence from unknown third parties, because they are more likely to travel to their visits by car, when things do go wrong in the countryside, they are often farther from immediate sources of help. Most research into violence and aggression indicates that the majority of it comes from clients who are often already well-known to services and from whom there have been previous indicators of risk (Brown et al., 1986; Poyner and Warne, 1986). Thus, workers should consider whether solo visits to isolated homesteads, to clients whom they may already have reasons to be wary of, are necessary.

One Warwickshire Social Services children and families team, whose visits often necessitated 60-mile round trips, routinely undertook joint visits for risk assessments and developed a practical enhancement to the usual signing-out system for monitoring evening visits, and which was also sensitive to issues of confidentiality for clients (Davis, 1999). The team's receptionist simply extracted the details of each worker's last visit of the day from the diary and provided the duty manager with a slip with the name of the worker, the worker's mobile telephone number, the name of the client and their address and telephone number, and the anticipated time of arrival back home. Social workers and their partners, or significant others, have a list of the duty managers whom they can alert if the worker has not returned home when expected. The duty manager then contacts the client, or if this fails, uses the worker's mobile number to ascertain their whereabouts. This system assures confidentiality by keeping the client-sensitive information with the manager and lodges the responsibility firmly with the manager rather than leaving workers' families to follow up any concerns. However, it should be recognised that joint visits, mobile telephones and checking in systems, while helping to manage the risks, do not eliminate them. Although home visits are often a source of important information about a client's situation, it is arguable that they are sometimes overused and in many cases could be replaced by information gathered and disseminated over the telephone, or by requesting or requiring clients to attend interviews and meetings at safer venues.

In smaller communities, when violence and aggression are already pre-eminent features of a situation, such as when working with women and children who have been subjected to 'domestic violence', the easier identification of the worker with those who are being helped, leaves the worker rather more exposed to risk than is usually the case in urban districts. The lack of protective anonymity can be problematic for workers who are well-known locally and who are more likely to be recognised and their home addresses, subsequently, more easily discovered. Agencies should be alert to the risks inherent in such situations and give thought to whom they deploy for particular tasks. Workers should be encouraged to assess risk for themselves and should not feel that they have no choice about risky referrals. More (1997), suggests that workers consider the following points when undertaking their assessment of risk:

- *Tasks*—what tasks do you have to do that might upset other people?
- *People*—do you work with individuals or groups whose behaviour might be unpredictable or unreasonable? Do they have a history of violence and aggression?
- *Places*—are some of the places where you work or visit risky or unsafe? Can anyone else see you. Can you leave safely. Are there other places to meet?
- *Times*—are there times that are more unsafe than others?

The most important factor which contributes to the likelihood of violence and is within a worker's own control, is their own behaviour. It is abundantly clear that inexperienced and poorly trained workers are much more likely to respond badly to the initial indicators of violence and so, often unwittingly contribute to the spiralling risk of aggression (Pugh, 1997c). Workers can sometimes compromise their own safety by taking procedural shortcuts, or by having unrealistic assumptions about what is expected of them. In many risky situations, if you have doubts about the circumstances then trust your instincts and withdraw. By leaving the situation you create further time and space in which to reconsider the situation and seek advice and support from other people (More, 1997). Risky situations typically arise when existing knowledge is not shared, when workers work alone in socially and geographically isolated settings, when clients are frustrated in some way by the agency, and when they receive distressing news, advice, or requests that they do not wish to hear.

Finally, while these points may be rather obvious, it is worth noting that the weather in rural areas is often harsher than in urban areas. Consequently, what would be minor difficulties in urban areas caused by heavy rain, or snow and ice, become more serious problems when one is several miles from the nearest main road on unlit and poorly maintained roads. Similarly, an unreliable car which is a nuisance in town, can present considerable problems when there is no other source of transport or assistance readily available. Good driving skills, a well maintained car, and footwear with good grip and additional warm, waterproof clothing are advisable. Employers should consider providing mobile telephones to improve communication and safety, but there are still localities where these do not work because of the lack of signal and the terrain.

Services to Children and Families

The implicit frameworks within which social workers make judgements about people, that is, their assumptions about how the world is and what sorts of people and problems exist within it, undoubtedly extend to the stock of ideas which they may hold about rural childhood. There is a risk that they may unwittingly subscribe to idealised representations and tend to see the rural child, as:

... an individual secure and important in his (sic) own right ... is closer to the natural world—of growing things, seed time and harvest, decay and renewal. Because of this he is quieter and usually more serene—somehow slower yet often more self assured, he is aware of belonging to something real, and what he sees in the countryside reassures him as to this knowledge.

(1978, Munro cited in Jones, 1997, p166)

This image of the rural child is clearly a simplistic stereotype, but it does raise the interesting question of what influence a rural upbringing has upon children. Although there are studies which examine how urban children fare in poor neighbourhoods, there is relatively little well-established evidence that would allow even qualified generalisations on the influence of the rural community context in regard to the formation of personal characteristics, or upon the quality of parenting (Simons et al., 1997). Moreover, such research is rarely conclusive for the direction of causes and effects is usually very difficult to establish.

In contrast, much of the British social work research on child care consists of single evaluative studies of rural projects, and apart from identifying those problems which arise from transport difficulties and lack of services, they hardly focus at all upon the social context of rural life. The contrast is clear when one looks at an Australian study of child abuse notification in a country town (Manning and Cheers, 1995), which attempted to identify how residents reacted to their suspicions of abuse and tried to identify the factors that influenced their decisions. This study found that:

- The decision to report was rarely taken alone, it was usually discussed within a person's immediate social network beforehand.
- Most reports were made by women, as it was widely felt that this was 'women's business'.
- Some who made reports preferred to remain anonymous for fear of possible repercussions from either the suspected abuser, or from the wider community. While others were willing to identify themselves since they thought that it was impossible to remain anonymous in a small town.
- There appeared to be a high level of concern expressed for children's welfare, and this possibly stemmed from a wider feeling of responsibility for their community.
- People were more willing to report suspicions of abuse when there was a local office or credible professional in their community, i.e. someone whom they might already have prior knowledge of, or who had a solid reputation.

The researchers suggest that:

In a small town where most people . . . would have some acquaintance with each other, most would know something about each other, and many would be related through kinship or friendship . . . then the chances of an abusing family with a good public image and one that is on friendly terms with a significant number of other residents, being brought to the attention of the authorities would be slim.

(Manning and Cheers, 1995, p388)

This research admirably attempts to situate the specifics of child abuse notification within the broader dynamics of a rural community, and makes some valuable suggestions as to what social service departments might do to promote notifications. Although it is not intended that readers generalise from this to other contexts, it is interesting to speculate whether similar dynamics might operate in British rural contexts? There is some possibility that they do, for the quotation mirrors a similar observation reported in the later section on 'domestic violence', where the factors that determine the community response are complex, but it seems that the extent of any support for an abused women is partly influenced by local perceptions of the abuser. While it is not unreasonable to suppose that the safety of children, or adults, at risk may be enhanced in small communities where there is a high level of shared social knowledge of people, we should be careful not to assume that this in itself is protective of them. The decision to intervene or report suspicions may be tempered by considerations of the risks to the person reporting if they are 'found out', which is much more likely to happen in small social networks, by perceptions of the abuser and the victim, and by perceptions of the potential response of the police and social services. Furthermore, there is a paradox in that while people in small communities which are geographically dispersed may well have considerable knowledge of other people in their locality, they may not see them frequently. Thus, there can be much lower levels of the sorts of informal surveillance and monitoring which occur spontaneously in other locations, as relatives, neighbours, and other professionals go about their daily business. Clearly, idealised notions about the nature of rural life, which may include the idea that child abuse is predominantly an urban phenomenon, can result in rather risky assumptions about the safety and vulnerability of children. Community education initiatives can raise awareness and help correct misconceptions about the 'official' response, while help lines, such as the Children's Rights scheme established by NCH Action for Children in North Wales, make it easier for children to seek advice and support, and to report their situation to others.

A discussion of the main issues around rurality and 'domestic violence' follows later, but it is important to note here the overlap between the abuse of women and the abuse of children. Mullender (2000), in a useful summary of how agencies might respond to the needs of children notes that the:

> ... overlap between women and abuse and child physical abuse is variously estimated at between 30 and 60 per cent. There is also a substantial overlap with child sexual abuse (nearly half the cases in one study) (and) up to one third of children on child protection registers live with domestic violence.
>
> (Mullender, 2000, p1)

The risks to children which may be overlooked if social workers do not realise the links between 'domestic violence' and child abuse, may be further exacerbated by relative isolation in rural areas. Moreover, in a UK context where few abused children are likely to receive appropriate help, the general absence of rural services to children makes it even less likely that they will get the help they need. As Mullender concludes, ' We are a long way short of the integrated, comprehensive coverage we need in the UK' (2000, p2).

One aspect of children's services in rural areas that has been well-researched is the shortfall in provision of pre-school child care, where demand for day care services such as nurseries and play groups is increasing (Cohen, 1995; Palmer, 1991; Statham and Cameron, 1994; Stone, 1990). Even when population differences are taken into account, the levels of provision are generally much lower than in urban areas and all-day care is usually difficult to find. The inequity in provision is not simply the result of the additional costs of rural provision, but also stems from significant differences in funding. For example, in 1991 'social service departments in the English shire counties spent an average of £18 per year on day-care for each child under five, compared to an average of £48 for English local authorities as a whole' (Statham and Cameron, 1994, p1). The lack of access to affordable and reliable child care remains a major obstacle to families who wish to improve their income through additional paid work, and also has an impact upon children's social and educational opportunities. Moreover, the absence of such services makes it more difficult for social service departments to provide support for families under stress and children at risk and those in need. The absence of provision can have significant knock-on effects in rural areas, and can be a further pressure upon younger families to move away. As Cohen observes, 'child care is not a marginal "add-on" for rural communities. It is fundamental to their future' (1995, p13).

Fortunately, awareness of the problems of scarce childcare is quite high, partly because all social service departments are required by the Children Act to undertake a joint review with education departments of their day care and educational provision for children up to the age of 8 years. However, a number of social service departments have developed more comprehensive approaches to encourage and increase levels of service. Powys County Council pioneered the extension of the definition of children in need under the provisions of the Act to rural children, by defining one indicator as, 'children whose development is significantly impaired by rural isolation' (reported in Statham and Cameron, 1994), and also developed, in partnership with the Save the Children Fund, a project to audit existing provision, to encourage new development and to co-ordinate planning among a wide range of statutory and voluntary organisations (Esslemont and Harrington, 1991; Powys Partnership Project, 1996).

Cumbria Social Services have tried to link their children's services plan to the Rural Development Strategy and other developments being undertaken within the local authority (Whittle, 1995). In 1994 they launched a Child Care Information Service which established a data base of existing provision and provided information via leaflets and a telephone help line. The data base is regularly updated and local directories of facilities are issued every six months to clinics, schools, libraries, doctors' surgeries, post offices and so on. This service contributes to the planning process by identifying gaps in existing provision. Cumbria also created a new post of County Training Co-ordinator for Childminders to audit training needs, and to support existing childminders through training and support, as well as promote the recruitment of childminders in areas where there are shortages. The third initiative they undertook was to establish Area Committees for the Under 5s, which have the task of preparing local strategies for developing local services and meeting unmet needs, which then contribute to the countywide plans. These committees have raised the profile of pre-school provision in the county and have formed the basis for joint planning and applications for development funding from other bodies. *Country Children Count* (ACC, 1995), the report of the joint conference organised by the Association of County Councils, the Kids' Clubs Network and the National Council of Voluntary Child Care Organisations provides a useful summary of issues around multi-agency partnership and joint working, and has many examples of innovative practice in developing after-school clubs, multiple use facilities, outreach workers for children in need, mobile facilities, and other peripatetic provision. In her review of childcare provision in Scotland, Palmer (1991), also provides some examples of creative responses from Scotland, as well as other European countries.

The relatively scarce and scattered nature of the rural population, combined with the problems of transportation, can make it very difficult for rural children to access services which would be readily available in urban areas. Furthermore, even when they can be accessed, rural children are often reluctant to participate in town or city-based projects. This has a number of unfavourable consequences, for example, vulnerable children may not have access to services which are aimed at preventing admission to care and accommodation. A Scottish initiative by Perth and Kinross Council and NCH Action for Children set out to divert young people from the legal and care systems by devising intensive 12 week individual programmes for the children and young people referred to their scheme. Each young person is allocated to a project worker who may work with them for up to ten hours each week. The programmes may comprise of group work, family sessions, individual counselling and other one-to-one work, located in the young person's home, school, or other convenient and appropriate local settings. A review of progress is held at the mid and end points, and some children may be then become involved in another programme cycle. Although this project targeted children from 12–16 who were having behavioural problems at school or were having difficulties establishing relationships with their age group, flexibility is central to their approach, and it has also been used with children as young as eight years. The project found that after the first year:

... that of 28 children with behavioural problems at school, 19 showed a marked improvement, six some improvement and only three showed no change. The success rate was even higher where child protection issues were involved, with 16 out 20 children showing a marked improvement.

(Mitchell, 1998, p29)

An evaluation of a self-help project for rural lone parents (Hooper, 1996), showed the importance of having a core person around whom the self-help groups could revolve. The project employed a part-time co-ordinator who established drop-in centres in a number of small rural towns in North Yorkshire and Humberside, and they also made home visits and provided advice and advocacy support by telephone. In this project, 93 lone parents made contact within the first three years, and 90 per cent of these were women. Rural isolation was very apparent in their circumstances, as 35 per cent had less than five regular contacts a week with other people, and a further 38 per cent only had between five and ten contacts per week. Fifty-two per cent of these lone parents were wholly reliant on public transport, and 27 per cent had no telephone. Poverty was, of course, a major feature in many of their lives with 77 per cent of them receiving income support. The parents' valued the social support offered by the project and the help with legal problems, and while there were variations in attitudes towards the project, 60 per cent described it as being 'important' or 'fairly important' to them. However, the assumption that the project worker would work intensively in one area to establish self-help groups and then partially withdraw and move onto another district, proved to be rather optimistic. In fact, users wanted more, rather than less, worker input and wanted it to be more continuous, so while volunteers were helpful, they had difficulty in 'establishing the legitimacy of their role within the groups ... Volunteers could supplement but could not substitute for the project worker's role' (Hooper, 1996, p4).

In their case for higher funding for public services in rural areas a Shropshire working group illustrated some of the difficulties facing their clients:

- A child with severe learning disabilities whose needs could not be met within mainstream schools might face a tiring 40 mile round trip to attend a special school.
- Specialist support such as speech therapy would only be available in term time at school.

- They would be isolated from school friends and other social activities might be limited by lack of transport.
- Occasional weekend respite care would also probably involve transport over some 20 miles.
- Social work visits to support the parents would be costly in staff time and travelling.

(Shropshire Regeneration Partnership, 1998)

This group noted that not only were staff and travel costs predictably higher because of distance and the fact that it was harder for social workers to organise their home visits as efficiently as in urban areas, but that costs escalated when a child was accommodated and it also cost more to maintain contact between them and their families. Interestingly, the Quality Protects objectives make specific reference to helping disabled children and their families live 'ordinary lives', so while this initiative is intended to promote the general safety and welfare of children, it does present an opportunity for families in rural areas to press for improved services and for agencies to seek better funding to meet the higher costs of provision.

Relatively little has been published about rural children in residential care, though the shift away from residential provision to foster care, adoption, or continuing support at home has reduced the likelihood of the accommodated rural child remaining within easy access of their own community. What is known, however, is that rural children leaving care are often further disadvantaged by their location, and some of the damaging and risky consequences are identified in the later section on youth homelessness. Despite the existence of much valuable guidance and advice (Biehal et al., 1995; Broad, 1999; Stein, 1991), many local authorities do not currently implement best practice in terms of preparing children for independent living or supporting them after they have left care. Furthermore, leaving care interviews, in which young people are routinely asked their opinions about the care they received and what continuing support they might like, and other arrangements for post-care help and keeping in touch, are generally notable by their absence. This woeful situation is currently being addressed in the Children (Leaving care) Bill introduced to Parliament in November 1999. The proposals will strengthen the obligations that a local authority has to young people in its care, as well as some of those it formerly cared for. Thus, it is likely that local authorities will be required to:

- Keep in touch with all care leavers.
- Develop personal pathway plans that will run at least until the young person is 21, which will address accommodation needs, as well as arrangements for career training, and further and higher education.

- Provide support with the costs of education and training up to the age of 24, whenever the course starts.
- Appoint advisers to help develop pathway plans and to monitor and implement them.
- Review the plans every six months or more frequently as needed.

While these proposals are aimed broadly at all eligible children, they will provide a framework which has the potential to better address the particular needs of rural children in regard to accommodation and continuing support. These proposals will only apply to children leaving care in England and Wales, though it is possible that the Scottish Parliament may adopt similar measures.

Community Care

From the inception of the National Health Services and Community Care Act (1990), scepticism was expressed about whether the assumption and expectation that communities were able and willing to provide the help and support necessary to enable the development of non-institutional provision for adults needing care services were realistic, reasonable, or even fair ones (Williams, 1989). In particular, the sexist assumptions that were implicit within the policy were challenged (Brown and Smith, 1993; Hooyman and Gonyea, 1995). While it is likely that at that time most social service departments probably had a more realistic picture of the capacities of the communities they served than the government, subsequent events have established the pitfalls of simplistic assumptions about what non-formal resources might be available. In fact, the shortcomings quickly became apparent when the National Council for Voluntary Organisation examined the community care plans of 39 English shire counties and found that only five made any specific reference to rurality in them (NCVO, 1994). Partly in response to this survey, the Social Services Inspectorate undertook a detailed inspection of community care in eight rural areas in 1998/9 and published the individual reports and an overall summary (*Care in the Country*, Social Services Inspectorate, 1999). The Inspectorate concluded that while over 'half of the English population aged over 74 live in rural areas . . . levels of service for people in rural areas was (sic) lower than for people with the same needs in urban areas' (SSI, 1998b, p1) and this was in a context where it was apparent, that, 'the more rural the district the greater the proportion of older people' (ibid., p5). The Inspectorate did not offer reasons for this unsatisfactory state of affairs, but it is likely that the powerful idealisations of rural life which were described in Part 1, may still have some effect upon perceptions of needs and services. Indeed, the Inspectorate suggested that 'The notion of *community* in rural areas may well mask the reality of social isolation and poverty for some people whose expectations of good quality services are low' (Social Services Inspectorate, 1998b, p5). Nonetheless, there is little doubt about the existence of a considerable potential demand for community care services. For example, Gant and Smith (1991), found that older people constituted 68 per cent of the 1400 casework referrals received by Gloucestershire Social services Department in 1984–5.

Some of the consequences of this neglect of rural services were revealed in a survey by the National Federation of Women's Institutes (NFWI, 1993), into rural carers in England and Wales. They found that:

- 42 per cent of them were full time carers
- 22 per cent cared for two or more people
- 33 per cent received no regular help
- 83 per cent of those over 65 lived with the person they cared for
- 38 per cent of the people they cared for were over 85 years
- carers tended to be older than their counterparts in urban areas (the average age being 60 years)
- over 50 per cent had developed health problems as a result of their care responsibilities

Clearly, this is a most unsatisfactory situation, as the prevalence of isolated and unsupported carers increases the potential risks for both parties. Carers may be more prone to stress and ill health, while those cared for may be more vulnerable to inadequate or even abusive care. Dalley's distinction between *caring for* and *caring about* (1988) helps our understanding of the reasons for the lack of support, and as Taylor notes, it:

> ... continues to be useful because it emphasises that caring involves both services for people who cannot provide such activities themselves, and affection which may also include the work of managing feelings and sustaining relationships. However, there are also risks in linking caring for and caring about because the latter can be romanticised ... (and) carers who care about are expected to be self-sacrificing and caring tasks are not seen as real work because they do not resemble the structured, time regulated work of the marketplace.
>
> (Taylor, 1999, p68)

Social workers need to challenge the assumption that women should and will provide informal community care and recognise that men may also provide care, and to accept that neither should be left unsupported and vulnerable simply because of their emotional attachment to the person they care for. The task, as Taylor notes, is 'to understand the conditions under which caring by women and men is undertaken and how it can be supported by formal services' (1999, p69). Consequently, the uncritical assumption of idealised notions of families and communities in rural areas is detrimental to this task, for it obscures the real scale of potential needs. Although the Carers (Recognition and Support) Act 1995 has introduced the right for carers to have their capacity and needs considered, it only applies when the person being cared for is actually being assessed under the provisions of the National Health Service and Community Care Act (1990), and misses those who remain 'invisible' as they undertake their caring work, maybe because they do not wish to bother anyone else or perhaps feel guilty about seeking help for themselves. Taylor reports the evaluation (Fischer et al., 1995) of a useful scheme to support carers which was piloted in rural south west England. This study found that carers especially valued:

• Contact, which acted as a form of psychological maintenance and reduced their feelings of isolation.
• Advocacy help, which made them feel that someone was 'on their side' in relations with other formal bodies.
• Assistance, in obtaining and providing practical services, such as picking up and delivering aids, prescriptions and so on.

Another interesting initiative in Norfolk is aimed at supporting elderly carers, and provides them with information about local services through an information sheet, a telephone help line, home visits from the project worker, and workshops on relevant topics such as safe lifting and managing incontinence. This work is also supported by volunteers trained to help and befriend the carers (Rickford, 1996).

The position of older people in rural areas is substantially affected by factors that have been noted earlier; poor transport, increasing centralisation of services, lack of awareness and poor service provision. As Age Concern reported:

Limited local facilities such as shops and transport make it harder for older people to remain independent at home but there are few statutory home care services. The provision of home carers and cleaners, meals services, day centres and aids and adaptations is relatively poor in rural areas ... There is some day care for older people in 8 per cent of parishes in rural England; 3 per cent have some provision for disabled people ... (which) tends to be in parishes with a population of more than 1,000 ... There is far less sheltered housing in rural areas compared with mixed and urban areas. When schemes do exist, they tend to be concentrated schemes in large villages or towns which can mean that older people have to leave their own communities.

(Pizey and Lyon, 1998, pp8–9)

120

In small communities and villages the social and the self-identity of older people is often bound up with perceptions of their domestic competence, and specifically, with the appearance of their homes. A study of the importance of 'low-level' preventive services to older people (Clark et al., 1998a) found that help with housework, gardening, home maintenance and repairs, all helped to enhance the quality of life for older people and helped them maintain their independence, and potentially reduced the need for more expensive and extensive interventions. The older people in this study wanted help not care, and they valued not having to always rely upon their families for support, but what they felt they wanted shifted according to changing circumstances and personal capacities. However, services were not always responsive enough to these changing needs, and the tendency of most social service departments to give priority to meeting personal care needs rather than domestic help, could lead to a mismatch between expressed needs and service provision especially for those older people who were not perceived as having higher levels of needs. In particular, the older women:

> . . . *saw the withdrawal of help with housework and related activities as a failure by social services to understand what was important to them. In their view, getting such help stood between staying in their own homes and going into residential care.*

> (Clark et al., 1998b, p3)

Despite the lack of 'official' recognition of the importance of housework in people's self-perceptions and the perceptions of their social competence, the study found that home carers understood these needs, and often went beyond their formal role and undertook extra domestic tasks for their clients. Perhaps the most significant aspect of the relationships between the home carers and the people they helped, was that they were typically seen as being friends, or 'like a daughter' (sic), and clearly helped to reduce feelings of loneliness and isolation. The implications for service development are obvious. Planners should rethink the prioritisation given to domestic services and where there is no local Care and Repair organisation that can provide a secure and trusted resource, they should consider developing one. A more flexible response to users' needs has been demonstrated by Bedfordshire Social Services who have offered people who refuse an offer of day care, three hours of home care support on two days a week, which the user can use as s/he wishes (Social Services Inspectorate, 1999).

The value that people attach to home care services is clear, but apart from the question of what sort of services are provided, there are some fundamental difficulties in providing such services in rural areas. A report into rural services cited two comments from service users which seem to epitomise their perceptions of home care services:

I cannot have appropriate carers. I have to accept who they send.

I cannot get help to go to bed in the evening.

(Social Services Inspectorate, 1999, p23)

These were not isolated problems, for the Inspectorate noted that most rural social services departments found difficulties in:

- arranging staff time efficiently
- staff recruitment and retention
- staff shortages leading to lack of choice for users
- providing replacements when staff were sick or on leave
- travelling time and travel costs were costly
- meeting users' concerns about confidentiality when staff were local
- meeting users' concerns about consistency of care, i.e. being helped by a known and trusted person

Some SSDs were having to recruit staff from outside of the locality, and some had organised 'bed runs' to help people get safely to bed, but the distances that had to be travelled increased the chances of delay and reduced the predictability of the service. There are no easy solutions to some of these difficulties. While local recruitment campaigns and better rates of pay may increase the availability of local staff, the higher relative costs of staff time and transport are a key issue in the less populated rural districts. Even the introduction of a rural premium in the Standard Spending Assessment, which would help social service departments meet the higher costs associated with the provision of rural services, would not in itself defuse users' concerns about confidentiality and privacy which may be exacerbated by increased local recruitment.

Nevertheless, there are some lessons that can be learned from the experiences of the SSDs that were inspected. Home care managers should routinely consult with service users about their preferences in regard to local staff, and always inform users of any delays or personnel changes. Some authorities allowed home care staff to use their meals on wheels delivery vehicles outside of the times that these were normally used, and some had encouraged home care managers to work from home, in the belief that this made them more accessible to users and more aware of local circumstances. Good transport practice observed in some departments that were inspected included; allowing extra time for journeys in bad weather and during harvest times when delays can be caused by slow moving machinery; being prepared to respond quickly to bad weather forecasts to ensure that people were picked up and delivered home again safely; and, expecting drivers who cannot get their vehicles to their 'pick-up' point in poor weather, to continue to the user's house and check that they are safe and have sufficient food and fuel (Social Services Inspectorate, 1999).

Instead of transporting the client, it is generally preferable to bring the service closer to the user but a dispersed and relatively small population of potential users, can make it expensive to provide more accessible locally-based services. A study into a day care project in a rural area of Northern Ireland (Gibson et al., 1995), which provided respite support for carers who had not previously received any services, found that with shared premises they did manage to keep costs down, but they also had some problems because of a lack of suitable secure storage for their equipment when other users of the premises were on site. Interestingly, this study found that while carers were very trusting and appreciative of the care provided, they showed little interest in knowing what actually went on in the day care centres. Gibson and her colleagues suggest that these 'high levels of satisfaction and low level of demand are typical of new service users in rural areas who have been unaccustomed to articulating needs or demanding assistance' (1995, p4).

Creativity and flexibility are key elements in maximising accessibility and choice for users and the Social Services Inspectorate have found instances where local authorities have used:

> ... home working to reduce travelling time for staff and increase their accessibility to service users. Some were developing the use of residential homes, sheltered housing, village halls and day centres to provide more and different services than they are primarily intended to provide. For example, some residential homes were diversifying to provide day care, short term breaks and various kinds of support outside the residential homes. The communal lounges of sheltered housing and village halls were sometimes used as bases for day care and other kinds of outreach support whilst day centres themselves were often endeavouring to provide a wider range of services than would ordinarily be associated with day care.
>
> (Social Services Inspectorate, 1999, pp7–8)

This type of flexibility should be encouraged, and one residential home in a small market town which I used to visit some twenty years ago had seen the opportunities that their situation offered. On market days, a succession of very old and generally rather frail, and sometimes rather unkempt, retired farmers would visit during the day to have a bath, receive chiropody services, get their clothes washed and mended, see the community nurse, have a meal, get their haircut, and so on. Usually, they would come into town on the weekly bus, or be ferried in by a neighbour or volunteer, though the staff would sometimes bring them in on their way to work. This approach provided valued physical services and social contact, an important opportunity for them to receive help and occasionally, for them to be admitted on a short term basis when they were ill. Sadly, much of this creative work came to an end when social services headquarters found out about it, and discouraged the staff from continuing to develop this 'open door' approach. In many areas of Wales, schools have long been used for multiple purposes and the ready access to transport, good catering facilities and a potential network of volunteers can sometimes be mobilised to create new sites for service provision. In some situations, the support and provision of payment to neighbours who are already providing informal services can make their continuance more likely. Local pubs can be recruited as providers of home meals, and instead of always delivering the meals, in Wiltshire, those recipients who are able to access the cafe or pub are encouraged to eat their meal there in company, rather than in isolation at home. However, such innovations should not be initiated at the expense of client choice, as Shropshire Social Services found that some users were unhappy about the type of food that was offered to them at their local pubs (Shropshire Regeneration Partnership, 1998).

Loneliness and the fear of isolation at times of difficulty are pressing concerns for some older people and a number of organisations have developed caller schemes which are mostly variations on two basic types of service. The first requires the user to initiate the contact and usually consists of them having a general number, or a specific person, to telephone when help is needed. In the second type, the call is initiated by the service itself, usually made by a person who is already known to the user, and who calls to see if they need assistance. Some help lines focus upon practical assistance while others provide social support and befriending. In some areas, the informal surveillance by local people can be encouraged simply by them having a known point of contact where they can report their concerns. Similarly, it can be helpful for potentially vulnerable people who may need help to know that local people can do this on their behalf, and thus remove some of the fears that they may have about burdening someone else with their troubles. There is much scope for redefining the expectations that people may have of how they should access services. For example, those who live alone and have no telephone could be encouraged to use local postal workers as a point of contact with local health and social services.

Unfortunately, the managerialism that has come to dominate the assessment and commissioning processes in community care services has led to a overwhelming concentration upon the practical services which may be offered and seems to have led to agencies ignoring or playing down the non-material needs of their clients. The Social Services Inspectorate, in a generally favourable report into Wiltshire's community care services, found that:

From the users we interviewed and the files we examined, there was some evidence that the psychological and emotional needs of service users were not always addressed directly as part of the assessment and care planning. We also saw some excellent work where these issues had been grasped. These differences seemed to arise from differences in care manager's practice.

(Social Services Inspectorate, 1998b, p12)

When the Wensleydale Mental Health Project in North Yorkshire researched the extent of unmet mental health needs in their area, they found 1,360 elderly people with mental health problems. Two-thirds were suffering from depression or anxiety-related conditions sufficient to warrant medical support, yet most 'were receiving little or no help, and isolation and loneliness were identified as major influences on their mental health' (Rickford, 1996, p26). The project's response was to pilot a health and social services joint-funded befriending scheme.

One recurrent problem is that many potential service users are unaware of what services and help they might call upon, and without adequate information, potential users may also lack sufficient information to make informed choices about the services they require. The Social Service Inspectorate's report into rural services noted that 'Innovations such as databases in libraries and advice centres tended to be located in towns' (1999, p9), and the distribution of other sources of information such as might be found in free local advertising papers, was often very limited in rural areas. Even shops and post offices did not display much information, though one Citizens' Advice Bureau had held sessions in a local GP's surgery, while others used advice workers who could visit people at home. Mobile offices, information displays, and the use of school IT facilities, might all provide useful ways of spreading knowledge about services.

It is difficult to generalise about the situation of adults with learning disabilities in rural areas, other than to acknowledge the lack of services geared to their needs and to note that they may have to travel considerable distances to access what is available. In many respects, it may be more difficult for them to integrate into geographically dispersed communities and transport difficulties compound the situation. Paradoxically, while they may have fewer opportunities to mix informally with the local community, they do not benefit from the nominal tolerance that comes from relative anonymity in urban areas, for they may be recognised and shunned in an intolerant community. Of course, individual situations vary greatly, and it likely that those who have had some of their schooling within local schools, or whose families are well-known and respected, may find better acceptance in adulthood. For those born into farming families, the nature of farm work traditionally provided some opportunities for employment, but the increasing mechanisation of farming has reduced the need for physical labour while increasing the need for the capacity to handle complex machinery.

Studies into mental health issues in rural communities identify similar difficulties. The following problems are typical:

- Public attitudes and ignorance about the nature of mental health problems associated with fear and hostility towards those suffering from them.
- Strong feelings of stigma associated with mental health problems, which reinforces isolation and also makes people reluctant to seek help with their problems.
- Greater vulnerability of women and members of ethnic minority groups.
- Difficulty in accessing services, due to long distances to the nearest provision and the absence of community based support services.
- Lack of information about what is available.

In 1997 Mind, the mental health charity, set up a project called *ruralMinds* funded by the Department of Health, with the aim of improving the social situation of those with mental health problems in rural areas and also of improving services to them. This project had two main areas of activity. The first focused upon developing better training and better information resources and established a national resources centre which includes a library and reference materials, and the development of a web site, the *ruralMinds network* (www. mind.org.uk), to facilitate the exchange of information and provide a contact list of individuals and organisations interested in mental health issues in rural communities. Although its focus is upon issues in England, much of the material is of more general use throughout the UK. The second area of activity was aimed at influencing the purchasing and provision of mental health services in rural areas, and this included advocating for better services in areas where existing provision was scarce. It also looked at developing joint initiatives with other organisations, and included a model integrated care project in South Shropshire. At the time of writing, this project has been running for nearly three years, but a full evaluation of its outcomes is not yet available.

For those with disabilities, access into community facilities may be restricted by lack of wheelchair ramps and other aids to mobility, while public transport, even where it is available, may not be adapted to the needs of people with disabilities. Although many of the issues about providing services for people with disabilities are similar to those regarding services to older people, their particularly poor situation should be noted. While lack of resources and scarcity of transport affects the mobility, social integration and opportunities of many residents in rural areas, it obviously impacts to a greater extent upon those with disabilities, and especially upon those who, even with the help of mobility allowances, are dependent upon other people to take them from place to place. For younger people with disabilities, this situation is exacerbated by the almost complete absence of any day care services, special housing and residential care for them. A survey of rural services conducted for the Rural Development Commission (Spilsbury and Lloyd, 1997) showed that fewer than 5 per cent of parishes had any special housing or day care services for them, and less than 10 per cent had any residential care. This survey also showed that the situation for older people was hardly any better in regard to day care, though there were slightly better chances in regard to accessing special housing and residential care.

Services to Travellers

Traveller is often used as a generic term to describe a variety of people and communities, although it is important to note that in Ireland the term 'traveller' refers to a distinctive community with a long history and a clear sense of personal and group identity. Often referred to as 'tinkers', they are an indigenous group, 'native to Ireland, unlike Gypsies who came to Europe from India over a thousand years ago' (Stewart and Kilfeather, 1999, p44) Within the rest of the British Isles, the term 'traveller' encompasses a variety of groups with a range of different self-definitions, including, Roma, Gypsies, New Age, and so on. However, in this discussion the term is used in a general sense, because despite their differences, these individuals and groups face some similar problems, both in regard to maintaining their general lifestyle, and in regard to particular problems which might be the province of personal social services. The general problems are well documented in Fraser (1995), and Hawes and Perez (1996), and include the failure to fully implement the provisions of the Caravan Sites Act of 1968 and the subsequent criminalisation of unauthorised camping in the Criminal Justice and Public Order Act 1994, which have created considerable difficulties in finding places to stay, and have contributed to widespread experience of harassment and social exclusion. Life chances generally are markedly worse than those of the wider population. For instance, among travellers in Northern Ireland, the average life expectancy is 11–15 years lower, and infant mortality rates are three times higher (Ginnety, 1993;

Stewart and Kilfeather, 1999). It is in this wider context of disadvantage, persecution, mistrust, hostility and insecurity that particular problems are manifested, and in some instances, directly created by external factors.

Cemlyn's (2000), study of social services' response to travellers has shown how semi-settled and nomadic lifestyles may be wittingly and unwittingly pathologised by the assumptions and expectations that agencies and workers may have about them. Many people whose notions of what constitutes a 'normal' and desirable lifestyle, have great difficulty in appreciating the extent to which travellers' preferred ways of living are exactly that, a preference, and a conscious choice, which they make. Instead, they often make stereotypical assumptions that poverty, or a reluctance to work, is the primary determinant of their situation. Without a good knowledge of how different groups operate, social workers will often impose their own meaning upon unfamiliar situations, and these almost invariably simplify the complexity of what is happening. For example, Boushel, in a study of child welfare, identified some of the strengths and weaknesses of Irish traveller communities, in which:

> ... traveller children are in some ways well-protected by their community's shared values of family life and close social interconnectedness ... (they) will go to great lengths to tolerate and ameliorate socially unacceptable behaviour by members of the group.

(1994, p185)

However, these closely linked communities combined with 'religious and cultural traditions place a high value on marriage, so there are fewer single parents than in the settled communities in which they live, and traveller women are less likely than other Irish women to have paid employment outside the home' (ibid., p186), means that when things go wrong 'the options facing vulnerable women and children within the traveller community are very limited' (ibid., p186). Consequently, traveller women who have experienced the general hostility and discrimination aimed at their communities are much less likely to seek help from social services and other public services.

Their wariness is justified, as in the past social services departments have sometimes separated children from their families on grounds that today would not be accepted under current legislation and they have not served travellers well in other respects. The Social Services Inspectorate's investigation into rural community care services concluded that 'the needs of travelling people seemed to be overlooked' (1999b, p8). Dalrymple and Burke note that the provisions of the Children Act 1989, embody principles that are more supportive of those whose lifestyles are not considered mainstream. The principles of minimal intervention, parental responsibility, partnership, and a requirement to consider cultural and linguistic background, as well as the wishes of children themselves, creates a potentially much more tolerant context within which decisions about service and intervention should be considered. Furthermore:

> ... *the definition of need in Section 17 of the Children Act 1989 means that some traveller children become eligible for its provisions because of the living conditions they have to endure as a result of poor amenities provided by local authorities.*
>
> (Dalrymple and Burke, 1995, p111)

Similarly, the Mental Health Act 1983 and The National Health Service and Community Care Act 1990 also require that the cultural background of a prospective client is properly taken into account. Sadly, as Cemlyn's research has shown, there are few signs of an improved relationship between state agencies and travellers. The problem is that the relationship between travelling people and social services is one framed by contradictory aims and policies. Cemlyn says that social services face 'the complex task of balancing new corporate and control responsibilities on the one hand and welfare and humanitarian considerations on the other' (2000, in press). She contends that the aim should not be to seek greater interaction between travellers and social services, but instead, social workers should acknowledge the conflicts that exist and recognise that many travellers have good reason to be wary of seeking their help. Social workers are frequently seen as a threat to their children, as well as to their lifestyle, as they have implemented and enacted assimilationist laws and policies (Acton and Mundy, 1997). 'The police have used social workers as a threat "If you don't do this we'll get the social workers to take your children away" ' (traveller cited in Cemlyn, 2000)

Cemlyn's study found that very few social service departments had any significantly developed policies on providing services to travellers, and that their response to issues concerning travellers could be characterised in one of five ways (1999):

- Crisis response—reacting only when an issue of child protection or juvenile justice arises, which tends to create greater risk of confrontation.
- Increased access—making changes to services such as family support to improve the likelihood of access by traveller families, e.g. outreach work, neighbourhood centres.
- Specialist provision—through the creation of specialist posts to further develop outreach provision, community development and to take a lead in improving the knowledge and skills of other social services.

- Corporate approach (1)—where there was an integrated and co-ordinated attempt to improve public services to travellers and which spanned the whole authority, i.e. where the underlying attitude might be characterised as being fundamentally tolerant.
- Corporate approach (2)—where the underpinning attitude is intolerant and the authority's response tended to be centred upon planning enforcement and the provisions of the Criminal Justice and Public Order Act 1994.

The stance that a social work department took towards its responsibilities in regard to travellers established the context within which social workers contributed to assessments and the degree of influence that their reports had in authorities' decisions regarding enforcement. Cemlyn found that:

> ... *where inter-agency procedures were unclear and there was little sign of a lead from social services management, either social workers were ill-prepared and sometimes resistant to taking on these assessments, or alternatively that completed assessments, especially those recommending a stay of eviction, had no impact on the corporate outcome. (In contrast) where ... social services took an inter-agency lead and an agreed procedure was developed, an assessment could lead to a more acceptable outcome for all concerned including travellers, and more effective management of conflict.*

> (Cemlyn, 1999, p25)

Of course, the reluctance of some social workers to undertake assessments might also reflect their perception of the oppressive nature of the processes they are being asked to participate in, and the extent to which their assessments will affect the outcomes of such decisions is not solely related to the level of inter-agency co-operation. In some authorities, it is possible that social services are a lone voice in calling for a more constructive dialogue with travellers, and will not have any wider support for their position.

There is a widespread lack of confidence and mutual trust between official agencies and travelling communities, but as noted earlier, this is not always based upon accurate information. An interesting study in Scotland by Duncan (1996), that looked at neighbours' views of official sites for travelling people some while after they had been set up, found that most householders had no specific complaints and that their earlier fears had not materialised. Most of the negative expectations and the earlier resistance to the development of the sites were informed by previous experience of illegal encampments. Some local businesses and farmers reported some problems, such as trespassing, uncontrolled dogs and parking, and most felt that they had had to be more vigilant in ensuring the security of their property. Local education authorities had usually provided some extra resources for the schools which received the travellers' children, and the children themselves had integrated well into them. The study concluded that well managed sites, set up with adequate space for parking vehicles, sufficient play space for children, and secure boundaries where necessary, could avoid most of the difficulties that had arisen. Even when travellers attempt to buy property and establish their own sites, the planning system militates against this. Hawes and Perez (1996), found that while the usual success rate for planning applications is about 80 per cent, for travellers it is only 10 per cent.

Social workers may lack knowledge of different traveller cultures and if their agency adopts a crisis response approach, they may be reluctant to intervene, either because they fear that they will be met with hostility, or more benignly, they assume that travellers will 'take care of their own'. One teacher reported in Cemlyn's study, perceptively noted that there was 'a fine line to tread' for 'problems that would be taken very seriously in the settled population are made allowances for with Traveller families' (2000). One area where difficulties and misunderstanding can occur arises from culturally different perceptions about what constitutes age-appropriate activities. Cemlyn notes that settled communities often express fears about the welfare of traveller children whom they feel are under-supervised, are in danger, or are being involved in unsuitable work activities, and cites Okely's observation that, 'in the late 20th century . . . the rationale for preventing Gypsy children from accompanying their parents and thereby learning their multi-occupations has been that they are exploited' (Okely, 1997, p72). The lack of contact between social workers and travellers, or contact that only comes when there is a crisis of some sort, means that travellers often lack information about what services might be available, and may be reluctant to seek help when they do not trust social workers and are fearful of the consequences of revealing problems to them.

Whether the inadequacy of services to travellers arises from ignorance, fear, or over zealous notions of protection, there is often an underpinning assimilationist assumption. This ranges from an apparently benign feeling that their lives would be a lot easier if they would just become a 'little more like the rest of us', through to outright hostility towards those who refuse to participate in the 'normal' life of the community and the belief that they should 'fit in' or forfeit their rights to make any claims upon the wider society. These ideas have been recently strengthened by the media reaction to the arrival of travellers as refugees and asylum seekers from Kosovo. It is vital that social workers become educated about traveller lifestyles and gain a better appreciation of the significant cultural differences that exist, as well as developing a broader understanding of the fallacies that are embedded in assimilationist perspectives on social difference (Cashmore and Troyna, 1983; Mason, 1995). Unless they do this, they will continue to fail to meet the legitimate needs of travellers, for as Cemlyn notes, 'While only a few travellers need social services support, it is essential that this is available in an accessible and helpful way, and that informed assessments are made' (1999, p25). In addition, Cemlyn suggests that a better response to the needs of travellers requires that:

• Traveller issues become included on the wider equality agenda as a matter of course, and that basic principles of anti-discriminatory, anti-oppressive practice and human rights are upheld.
• Efforts are made to engage with traveller communities to establish their views and needs, and to promote mutual understanding and trust.
• Social services departments establish clear polices and take a stronger role in determining the broader policy of the local authority, especially in regard to the provision of sites and access to facilities such as laundries, and other services.
• Social services need to develop better inter-agency and multi-agency procedures.
• Social workers should be prepared to act as advocates for travellers in their dealings with other services, and provide support and advice in countering harassment and racism.
• A wider non-pathologising approach is taken to determining children's needs and that a preventive approach is taken to promote family support and community development.
• Statutory social services should support voluntary sector organisations who will usually find it easier to make links and provide services.
• Outreach work and specialist liaison workers can provide travellers with better information about the availability of services and promote a better understanding of issues within statutory departments.

Youth Homelessness

While awareness of homelessness in urban areas has increased considerably over the past few years, as sellers of the 'Big Issue' have become commonplace and the visibility of rough sleepers more apparent, there is not the same appreciation of the problem in rural areas. Consequently, the government's policy on rough sleepers is predominantly urban in focus, for as with many other rural problems, it is the reduced visibility that leads people to assume that there are few difficulties in this respect. A study in rural North Yorkshire showed that young people found it very difficult to find a job *and* somewhere to live (Rugg and Jones, 1999). While many young people would prefer to stay in the countryside, their experiences varied greatly and though most were in employment, they felt their prospects were often limited in terms of pay and advancement, and many remained far longer in their parents' home than they would have liked to. Some community councils have attempted to respond to these difficulties by developing Wheels-2-Work projects to help young people to access employment in rural areas by providing mopeds for them to travel to work. But, for those who lack work and accommodation, their homelessness exposes them to similar risks to their counterparts in urban areas—loneliness, vulnerability, poor health, crime, and abuse. A study of rural homelessness undertaken by Gunner (1999), for Centrepoint stated the problem:

> *When it is time to leave home or leave care young people in rural Devon face a difficult choice. They can stay near home, where people and places are familiar, or they can move away to an area where there are homes and jobs but little prospect of being able to afford to return to the countryside to live and work . . . finding a place to live is hard . . . some . . . as young as 16 or 17 years old . . . move from place to place, stay with friends until their welcome runs out, sleep rough and seldom come to the attention of anyone who might be able to help.*

(Gunner, 1999, p2)

There are numerous causes of homelessness among young people but some of the most prominent factors are: job shortages together with poor transport networks, low income, lack of affordable accommodation, disrupted ties with families, and leaving care. Although there is no reliable evidence of the scale of the problem throughout the UK, it is likely that what is happening in Devon is not untypical of other areas of the country, but it is harder to establish the extent of rough sleeping, for example, in dispersed and more scarcely populated areas than in cities and towns. Like so many other issues, the first step is simply to raise people's awareness of the possibility of the problem in their 'patch' and to understand their statutory responsibilities in regard to vulnerable young people. As Gunner points out, the general responsibility is very clear:

> *. . . every social services authority has a duty to provide accommodation for any 'child in need' who has reached the age of 16 and whose welfare is likely to be seriously prejudiced without accommodation.*

(Children Act 1989, Section 20)

Furthermore, the Act contains a specific duty to 'advise, assist and befriend' any young person up to the age of 21 who has previously been 'looked after' by local authorities (section 24). There is also a very clear policy steer being given to statutory social services to fulfil their obligations being promoted by initiatives such as the Quality Protects programme for managing children's services. In contrast, the Housing Act 1996 which only includes those over 18 years of age as being potentially eligible for public housing excludes those 16 and 17 year olds who might be most vulnerable when homeless.

Centrepoint have developed a strategic approach to tackling youth homelessness developed from their work in three rural counties—Devon, Oxfordshire and Warwickshire—which could provide a model for other areas. There are four main stages in their approach:

1. Gathering the facts—what is the nature of homelessness amongst young people, how many need somewhere safe to live, and what services are already available or being planned?
2. Consulting with interested parties, including service providers and organisations who worked with young people, and young people who had experienced difficulties in finding somewhere to live.
3. Consolidating the information into a report and developing mechanisms for partnership, planning, and policy development to devise a strategy for action.
4. Specifying the strategy, which included the following priorities— preventative measures (such as providing young people of school leaving age with realistic information about what leaving home and living independently entailed); emergency provision to ensure that no young person had to sleep rough; continuing interim accommodation and support for independent living; and developing affordable accommodation for independent living.

Gunner's report provides useful advice on how to undertake each of these stages and is a valuable source for any agency seeking to develop a more coherent local approach to homelessness among young people. One practical innovation was the introduction of deposit bonds to help young people secure rented accommodation. Although the study does not provide a clear cut evaluative summary of the project's performance, it is clear from the descriptive account that they have had some success in achieving their aims, especially in regard to educative and preventative measures, developing support services and encouraging interagency co-operation. Gunner identifies eight factors which contributed to this. They were:

- A commitment from senior managers to the research and the subsequent recommendations.
- Getting the best available data.
- Setting clear priorities and targets.
- Partners having a genuine commitment to adopt and implement the strategy.
- Continuing involvement by Centrepoint.
- Effective partnerships between young people and organisations in public and independent sectors.
- Heightened local awareness of problems and needs, especially through media coverage.
- The role of Centrepoint in acting as a catalyst to stimulate interest and provide resources to support the development of the project.

However, it should be noted that the wider context within which such problems are situated also needs to be addressed, and it is significant that among the recommendations arising from this project are several which are addressed to regional authorities and national government. These focus upon the discriminatory effects of minimum wage legislation, the benefits system and housing regulations, as they apply to those under 25 years of age, and also upon the need for planning and development authorities to be proactive in developing strategies to promote employment opportunities and access to suitable housing and so avoid homelessness in the first place. In her concluding evaluation Gunner notes that most people thought that there was a number of continuing roles that Centrepoint needed to play to keep the project going, since, as one social services manager said 'I don't think anybody else would have had the time to develop and promote this way of working . . . their contribution has been invaluable' (Gunner, 1999, p33).

Responding to Racism

Part 1 illustrated the continuing presence of racism in rural areas and showed how it is often linked to ideas about nationalism and 'who belongs' there. When the countryside is predominantly seen as a 'white' space, a perception that hides the 'growing presence and increasing recreational participation of people of colour' (Ageyman and Spooner, 1997, p197), then it is hardly surprising that anti-racism is often absent from policy making and planning for services in rural areas. Herman Ousely, the Chair of the Commission for Racial Equality, was moved to state 'that the colour-blind approach prevalent in rural areas is no longer acceptable, as it has failed to tackle racism, (Henderson and Kaur, 1999, p9). Moreover, it is clear that many agencies in rural areas are not meeting their responsibilities under the Race Relations Act 1976 and are reluctant to provide funding for local Race Equality Councils (Dhalech, 1999). While recognition of the existence of racism in rural areas is now more widespread, there is not yet an accompanying level of knowledge about the means by which racism might be tackled. A useful source of information on community based responses is published by the Community Development Foundation (Henderson and Kaur, 1999), which reports on projects undertaken in Cornwall, Devon, Somerset, Lincolnshire, Northern Ireland and Scotland.

One of the best examples is the Rural Race Equality Project undertaken between 1996 and 1998 in Cornwall, Devon and Somerset which is also available as a more detailed report (Dhalech, 1999). This report contains useful appendices, including incident report forms, guidelines for dealing with the media, and examples of the information sheets that were developed. This project arose from the report by Eric Jay entitled *Keep Them in Birmingham: Challenging Racism in the South West* (1992), when the National Association of Citizens Advice Bureaux together with the Rural Development Commission (now superseded by the Countryside Agency), decided to develop a pilot project to develop 'race equality policies and action' in the region. This was intended to act as a model which other agencies could use and develop elsewhere. The project was started in a climate in which it was widely assumed that there was no problem of racism, but it quickly became apparent that official bodies, such as the police, had little knowledge of the realities faced by ethnic minorities. 'The general belief ... was that there were no black people, no racism—in short, no problem' (Dhalech, p13 in Henderson and Kaur, 1999). This erroneous belief even extended to some of the bureaux in the region who did not participate in the project. Among its aims, the project was trying to:

- identify what black people expected from the Citizens Advice Bureaux
- find out what the barriers to effective services were, and to surmount these
- work with other agencies (statutory and voluntary) to improve advice services
- develop feedback on black people's experience of services
- evaluate the impact of the project

In fact, as Dhalech candidly admits, these aims were found to be too ambitious given the realities of existing circumstances and the prevailing attitudes within major local agencies. Very quickly, the project team realised that they would have to develop a more holistic approach than they had originally envisaged, largely because of the widespread ignorance and denial of the existence of racism in the region. Consequently, one of the first things that they did was to establish a reporting system to record racist incidents, and this became the 'most compelling answer to those who say we have "no problem here" ' (Dhalech, 1999, p4). The reports that were received demonstrated that discrimination was occurring in virtually every aspect of everyday life—in local shopping, in leisure and social activities, and in public services like housing, education, and social services. This 'invisibility' is a typical feature of racism in rural areas (Craig et al., 1999).

The other main initiatives of the project were to discover what relevant resources already existed within the area and compile these into a directory of useful contacts; to disseminate information through publicity, networking and the development of appropriate materials; to develop partnerships with particular bodies to improve existing work, or initiate new approaches, and to help establish support networks. The directory was one of the most valuable pieces of work and was very popular. The dissemination of information was undertaken using the web, newsletters, posters, leaflets, sympathetic local media, and one-off events, such as a conference, and by contributing to training and awareness raising in schools, colleges and youth clubs. Training and publicity events were often practical forms of partnerships with public services including the police, prison and social services, but there were difficulties in establishing any links with some organisations, and in developing partnerships into broader aspects of policy development. For example, one local authority officer's response to an approach by the project was:

> ... *we do not see ourselves as being able to be seen as supporters of your Project. However, if this were to cause a political embarrassment ... if we were to stick to a 'business-like' line, please do get in touch with me.*
>
> (Dhalech, 1999, p17)

This cynical response indicates a fundamental difficulty in many organisations that lack a corporate approach to racism, in that it is simply left to individuals to decide whether or not to participate or contribute in initiatives. While this may have some benefits, particularly at a grass roots level in allowing particular individuals the leeway to get involved—and often such individuals made a considerable contribution—it leaves new developments highly vulnerable to shifts in personnel and fails to secure the support of those senior managers and local politicians who decide priorities and allocate resources. In such circumstances, even where partnership of some kind is established, it can still be undermined by an institutionalised racism that makes no commitment to the basic principles of partnership, and by the thoughtlessness, ignorance, and personal racism of individual workers. For example, Dhalech reports that one agency exploited the knowledge and experience of minority ethnic professionals and race equality agencies by consulting with them to develop their guidelines, and then not acknowledging their contribution publicly, nor including them in further implementation and development. However, other examples of partnership were more productive. They contributed to the social work and social care training courses in local colleges, and also worked with educational providers by providing workshops for 16 year olds at a Human Rights Day event.

One aspect of this project which mirrors the experience of others, is the need to develop support networks for workers. This ranged from supporting the project worker/s in terms of explicit policies and procedures, especially around issues of personal safety and personal and professional support in what was often exhausting and challenging work, through to establishing networks of black employees in social services and probation.

Perhaps the most striking feature of the project was that it indicated how the everyday experience of black people in rural areas is part of a cycle of discrimination which results in poor levels of provision and continuing disadvantage:

• The isolation of living in rural communities with little or no support can exacerbate the experience of racism but maintain its invisibility.
• This in turn creates a lack of confidence to seek advice and information.
• As a result, minority ethnic community members are inclined to attempt to resolve the issues within the private circles of family and friends.
• This then emphasises their lack of awareness of what services are available to the public.
• Under-use of services and underreporting of the needs of minority ethnic people are often reinforced by previous negative experiences with an agency.
• As a result, developing confidence in communities that have continually experienced disadvantage and discrimination is a lengthy process and requires the long term commitment of human and other resources.

(Dhalech in Henderson and Kaur, 1999, p14)

Dhalech summarises the impact of the project so far:

It has been a long and slow process, requiring a great deal of patience and resulting in many disappointments. We have made progress, although some agencies appear just to have learnt to use the right language. The main issues are policy development, implementation, training and the development of confidence in minority ethnic communities.

(Dhalech, in Henderson and Kaur, 1999, p21)

Clearly, changing attitudes is always likely to be slow work, but this issue of confidence among the minority communities is an aspect of challenging racism that is not always fully acknowledged. Many of those who suffer racism, or would benefit from services, especially in rural areas, are reluctant to seek help or 'make a fuss' because they fear that in drawing attention to their problems and needs, they may be blamed for their own situation, or even worse, may become the subject of further discrimination, perhaps even violence. As de Lima observes, 'there is often a reluctance to become involved in any initiative which they feel would focus attention upon them as individuals, and they are often not keen to discuss their experiences of living in communities' (1999, p37). Workers seeking to develop responsive policies and services should be careful to recognise how significant this reluctance is. For although it may be a reasonably successful strategy for 'not being noticed', it may also represent a considerable degree of anxiety and fear about exposing themselves. It reminds us just how fragile and contingent the appearance of tolerance may be in a community. Racism, like other forms of discrimination, is never likely to be eradicated, and it may always remain a potent set of ideas and symbols that can be mobilised and used to damaging effect. One response, suggested by de Lima (1999), is to form links with ethnic minority groups by working with organisations who would not usually be associated with community development. For example, a Chinese language course for Chinese children in the Highlands helped the children maintain confidence in their bilingualism, and brought parents together as they transported their children to and from the classes.

In 1988, a report from the Social Services Inspectorate report, *Social Services in a Multi-Racial Society* stated that:

> *It appeared to be a matter of debate whether staff were more hampered in their contacts with black and minority ethnic communities by what they did not know about them or by what they thought they did know.*
>
> (Social Services Inspectorate, 1988, p14)

While there may still be good reasons for wondering whether things have changed much since then, there is little doubt that:

> *Staff working in rural areas are likely to get relatively little experience of working with minority ethnic service users. This makes it particularly important that they have access to specialist advice and support when they need it.*
>
> (Social Services Inspectorate, 1999b, p49)

While this is a useful suggestion, all staff should be prepared to consider the issue of how they work with people who are different from them.

Domestic Violence

This section is not intended to provide general guidance on how to respond to 'domestic violence', as this is better provided by other authors (Mullender, 1996; Home Office, 2000) but rather it aims to review the extent to which rurality is a relevant dimension of it. While the phrase 'domestic violence' is in many ways an inadequate way of naming and identifying the forms of male violence and aggression that are enacted towards women in abusive relationships and situations, it has the sole merit of being widely recognised as referring to what is also known more directly as 'woman battering' or 'spousal abuse' in the USA. Nonetheless, without entering into the wider debate, the phrase is used here with some reservations, especially in regard to its rather indirect quality which plays down the fact that, for the most part, it refers to violence directed by men to women and their children. The British Crime Survey (Mirlees-Black, 1999), in England and Wales found that over their lifetime, 22.7 per cent of women and 14.9 per cent of men reported that they had been the victim of a domestic assault. However, women were much more likely to have been significantly injured, to have suffered multiple assaults, and to have suffered threats and fear and anxiety than men. Furthermore, women are much more likely to be killed by their partners, with 47 per cent of female homicide victims, compared to 8 per cent of male victims. So we should not assume that there is any symmetry in the incidence or extent of violence between men and women, and the evidence overwhelmingly shows that women are much more likely to be hurt by men (Dobash et al., 1992).

It is unlikely that the causes of domestic violence in rural areas are essentially any different from urban areas, for it is a phenomenon underpinned by a raft of paternalistic and misogynistic assumptions about men and women's roles and relationships which spans the whole of British society. However, there are some important considerations in terms of how the rural context bears upon the experience and the response to domestic violence. As with so many other aspects of rural life, the relative social and physical isolation of individuals, together with the apparent invisibility of the problem, creates particular difficulties for those who suffer such violence, and for those who seek to help them.

The social and physical isolation of women in some areas may be exacerbated by men who are trying to control their behaviour and the contact that they have with others. The sense of being alone and powerless, which may be made worse when they are afraid to use the telephone, perhaps because the social services or Women's Aid number would show up on an itemised bill, or when they are prevented from using it because their partner takes the telephone away with him when he leaves the house, is probably stronger in isolated homes where visitors are even less likely to call unannounced than in similar situations in cities, and where there are fewer opportunities for casual contact with other people. Threats of violence, perhaps that 'no one will hear you here', are even more credible when the nearest neighbours or public telephones may be miles away. Isolation contributes to invisibility and signs of physical harm and distress may go unnoticed simply because there is no one else around to see them. The ready access to guns means that they are more likely to be used as threats, and in actuality, than in urban areas, and the slow response times of the police if a women needs immediate help may add to her sense of isolation. When a woman tries to seek help or escape the situation by leaving, she may not have access to a car at all, and if she does, her partner might have temporarily disabled it so that she cannot use it. She may not be able to use a local bus where there is no service, or what there is, is infrequent. Even if there is a bus she can use, the driver may recognise her, and calling a local taxi carries the same risk of recognition in small communities.

Like other problems in rural areas, the apparent invisibility of abuse lends weight to those who wish to deny or minimise the fact that there is any problem with domestic violence in their area. Often, such problems are perceived as being caused by incomers rather than by locals. Paradoxically, this parochialism is inverted when it comes to financial support for a local women's aid group, who may find themselves having to demonstrate that they are helping local women as well as those from 'away'. Such parochial attitudes, which are reminiscent of the old poor law, indicate a failure to understand the problems of domestic violence in rural areas. In the countryside, where people's knowledge of each other may cover a large geographical area, a woman's safety may only be assured by her moving some distance from her home area. Unlike the compartmentalisation of areas that occurs in large cities, safety and anonymity cannot be so easily established by a move of only a few miles. Thus, in a rural area, escaping to the nearest refuge which may be many miles away can disrupt other potential sources of support that a woman might have among her friends and community.

Homelessness is a common problem for women fleeing violence, and finding other suitable accommodation can be very difficult in dispersed rural areas, especially without private means of transport. The response of the surrounding community may not be predictable or consistent. In situations where the woman is a local and the man is an incomer, or he is perceived as being an outsider or different in some way, then local help and support may be forthcoming, but when the man is someone with some standing in the community, there may be considerable reluctance to acknowledge what is happening. Even when recognition occurs, or the circumstances are different, some of the community may implicitly, or explicitly, rationalise it by 'victim blaming', especially if the local culture is one that disapproves of divorce and separation. One Irish woman said, 'My family did not contact me for a year after I left my ex-husband. There is a tremendous stigma in being separated' (MacKay, 2000, p12).

Women from ethnic minority groups face additional problems in getting appropriate help. MacKay has noted how 'the assumption is often made that because domestic abuse crosses all racial, ethnic and class boundaries, every woman's experience of it must be the same' (2000, p16), whereas help-seeking patterns vary culturally and are also modified by the woman's particular context. Women from traveller families may be extremely reluctant to seek help from formal agencies which they regard as alien to their community, while Indian and Chinese women are less likely to seek informal help within small tightly-knit ethnic communities. In minority groups where women's status is strongly linked to that of their partner, there may be strong pressure not to 'go outside' to seek help as this may bring the group into disrepute, or cause shame. For women who do not speak English the risks of help-seeking may seem insurmountable, for gaining access may be beset with problems (Pugh, 1998). As MacKay notes, even attempting to seek help might 'expose women to culturally alien agencies and refuges, if not institutional racism . . . (and) the interpreting service may pose risks as well as a lack of understanding' (2000, p16). For example, untrained voluntary interpreters may be reluctant to convey information which they feel discredits their community, and may even exert pressure directly upon the woman to conform to their cultural expectations (Pugh, 1996). Problems can also occur when women from minority groups face racism within refuges as there is unlikely to be easy access to another refuge better able to meet their needs.

Probably the most important issue for those seeking to provide assistance to women who are subject to violence in their own homes, is to raise awareness of the services that they offer. This can often usefully be undertaken by working through existing points of contact between women, such as Mothers' Unions, play groups, and the WI. East Fife Women's Aid provide a useful review of the pros and cons of different ways of getting the message across, which includes—information articles, leaflet drops, stickers, publicity on tickets and receipts, posters, advertising, talks, discussions with other agencies, and participation in zero tolerance campaigns (MacKay, 2000). However, because many rural areas have more than one area telephone code, help line numbers that appear to be 'out of area' may be off-putting to potential callers. Small voluntary groups who receive requests for their services by telephone, should consider how best to organise their response. Savigear provides some general advice as to how voluntary organisations might do this when resources are scarce. Obviously, some of these suggestions are inappropriate for the services that Women's Aid groups usually provide, but it helps to focus attention upon the practicalities of how to organise telephone-based referral systems. The alternatives are:

- One telephone number at an office where personal contact can be made during advertised hours and messages left on an answer phone for the remainder of the time.
- One telephone number is used and calls are transferred to the person 'on duty'.
- One telephone number is linked to an answer phone. The message is changed to give the telephone number of the person 'on call' at the time. The person requesting help has to make two calls but gets a personal response to the second call.
- Several telephone numbers are listed, with each person taking responsibility for general duties. If no answer is obtained from the first call the client tries another number. It is inadvisable to list numbers vertically as the first person of the list will tend to receive the most calls! Printing the numbers in a circle as the spokes of a wheel will produce a more even load.
- Several telephone numbers are listed; each relating to a particular area of need such as transport. This can put a tremendous burden on individuals who may feel guilty if they are not available 24 hours a day!

(Savigear, 1996, p17)

In the more remote areas, making people aware that there is a service is even more of a problem, and as one worker said, 'There's nowhere to put information . . . (but) . . . if you want to put a notice on a cow or a sheep then you'll be alright' (MacKay, 2000, p9).

One enduring difficulty for many women's aid groups is of finding a balance between publicising a service and actually meeting the needs that it reveals when their funding is limited. Distance and transport difficulties combine to make access difficult, and impossible in some cases. In East Fife, the local Women's Aid group estimates that it would take a woman around two hours each way to travel in from the farthest localities in their area. If they have to take children to and from school or play group and are unable to call upon help from neighbours or friends, then it may simply not be possible to come in to town, seek advice and travel back again, in the time available. Moreover, if their oppressor is monitoring their movements then there is little chance of being able to be away from home for an 'untypical' amount of time. Many aid groups use outreach work as a way of reducing these difficulties, and while these can work very well indeed, some women will find it difficult to make and keep arrangements for a meeting when they are subject to the arbitrary terrorisation and restrictions imposed by their unstable partners. Another useful approach is to provide additional drop-in centres out in the smaller market towns which reduce travel distances and times, and where women can visit without any need for a prior arrangement. These centres should be sited discreetly, and ideally, in buildings where the purpose of a visit is not apparent simply by the fact of entering it. Multipurpose centres which contain other services and other enterprises are often most anonymous in this regard. The additional expense of providing outreach support and local centres adds considerably to the cost of services in dispersed rural areas. Sometimes, these can be reduced by using the premises of another organisation for regular 'surgeries' rather than providing a permanent facility. For example, some women's aid groups use Citizens Advice Bureau offices, while health centres and some commercial premises have also been used in this way.

Though most social service departments realise the benefits of working closely with local women's aid groups, and are beginning to recognise how violence to women is linked to harm to their children also, there can be difficulties in developing expertise and understanding of the problems of domestic violence, especially when generic workers have relatively infrequent contact with such cases. Ignorance of the dynamics of abuse and of the fear that it engenders can result in inappropriate advice and responses. This can extend to other professions too. For example, local solicitors who deal in general legal practice may lack specialist knowledge and not know how best to use the law to protect women. They may also not realise how their own position, and the woman's perception of it and the local knowledge that they also have, may be a disincentive to seek their services. The usual introductory small talk of first meetings in the countryside—'do you know so and so?', 'ah, my kids go to that school'—may not be seen as friendliness but as a potential threat to confidentiality. The worker's own position is also something that requires consideration in regard to confidentiality and personal safety (see earlier discussion).

A summary of the general implications of the review of joint working initiatives between women's aid groups and statutory bodies undertaken by Hague (1999), was noted earlier in Part 2, but two specific points are worth noting separately. Hague et al. (1996), found that the commitment of time and other resources by small organisations to multi-agency initiatives had sometimes led to already scarce resources being diverted away from direct service provision, and in some instances, resulted in a reduction in the level of emergency help available. Hague stresses that:

> *If interagency work becomes a talking shop and does not lead ... to improvements in women's and children's safety and to positive developments in services and policy ... then there would seem to be no point in bothering with it.*
>
> (Hague, 1999, p97)

Many small voluntary agencies would empathise with this point, for those who are committed activists, it is especially galling to feel that one's own direct knowledge and experience is being marginalised or wasted. Thus, it is vital that the statutory sector makes strenuous efforts to understand and 'hear' what is being said, and understands the opportunity costs that may be involved. In the same way that user participation should not be assumed to be a 'no cost' strategy, consideration should be given to facilitating the participation of smaller organisations by costing in the reimbursement of their time and other expenses. Otherwise, as one US study on rural interventions concluded:

> *The dependence upon volunteers can be seen as reflecting the poor funding available to these programs and as a reflection of society's devaluation of women in general and battered women's problems in particular.*
>
> (Edleson and Frank, 1991, p549)

Additional useful advice on developing multi-agency responses to 'domestic violence' can be found in Hague and Malos (1996), Hague (2000), and on outreach work generally (Kelly, 2000), but the most useful review of the issues regarding rurality and domestic violence is provided by MacKay (2000) in her report for East Fife Women's Aid. She summarises the main needs of abused women in rural areas as follows:

- knowledge that a service exists and what it provides
- access to locally based services
- outreach provision for those who cannot access the usual services
- a truly confidential and one-stop service, to avoid multiple contacts with different agencies
- a choice of refuges to meet individual needs
- continuing support after settling into a new home
- a proactive response towards the needs of all of the victims of abuse, including children

Drug Misuse

Rather belatedly, there has been a realisation that drug misuse is not solely an urban problem but is an issue in rural life too. Over the last few years, media stories, usually with a story line that involves the intrepid reporter discovering that even in deepest England or remotest Wales or Scotland illicit drugs can easily be purchased if one knows where to look, have begun to raise public awareness of the problems. Henderson reports some unpublished work by Leitner and Shapland undertaken for the Home Office, which suggested that country people underestimate the amount of drug misuse in their areas, but were 'less likely to consider cannabis, and to a lesser extent other drugs, harmful and more likely to view economic and social problems as causes of drug use rather than "fun seeking" ' (2000, p13). Lately, official bodies have begun to respond to this developing awareness, but it is only comparatively recently that they have 'recognised that the majority of research, prevention initiatives and models of good practice were urban by default' (Henderson, 2000, p12).

In 1998 Henderson was commissioned to 'map the broad social context of drug use and identify models of good practice by evaluating (existing) rural projects' (2000, p12), supported by the Home Office. She found that she could not establish any conclusive picture of rural drug use, and it was not possible to identify particular patterns of use, or whether levels of drug use were higher or lower than in urban areas. What did seem reasonably certain was that most local studies in rural areas found that about a quarter of all young people up to 15 years of age had either been offered illicit drugs or had actually used them. Furthermore, the misuse of veterinary drugs, owing to the relative ease of access to them on farms, is one aspect that clearly differs from urban areas. Henderson found that rural people had low expectations of the availability or extent of drug misuse services, and there were few locally based voluntary projects. Consequently, new projects originating from external bodies may be unwelcome because they force locals to acknowledge that there is a problem in their communities. Furthermore, potential supporters and volunteers may be reluctant to offer help if they think that their involvement may have a stigmatising effect upon them. Henderson suggests that such resistance is best overcome by working with existing local organisations, such as rural community councils, and linking with other concerns that a community may have about young people's alcohol consumption, community safety, family problems, disruptive public behaviour, and so on. Establishing networks and a base of support is crucial, otherwise project workers, many of whom work alone, may find themselves isolated, and have to carry the burden of being seen as the person 'responsible' for everything to do with drugs. She makes the point that such approaches should not be confined to rural communities, but should be used in any community or neighbourhood where people share some notion of 'place' or locality, rural or urban:

> *Close knit, inward looking communities where 'everyone knows everyone else' or can link you with your family, are less likely to acknowledge drug issues to 'outsiders' or seek help than more disparate, individualised ones.*

(Henderson, 2000, p15)

The essence of her position is that 'we need to fine-tune our sensitivities to cultural differences and similarities. Considering local realities rather than making universal assumptions' (2000, p15).

The situation in regard to our knowledge about alcohol misuse in rural areas is a little better, but there are some surprising gaps. While there is widespread recognition of the potential health risks and of the problems of alcohol related crime, such as drink driving and public disorder in rural villages and towns at weekends, the links to 'domestic violence' and child abuse are not as well known. In fact, there is very little data at all upon the extent of alcohol misuse in the countryside (All Party Group on Alcohol Misuse, 1995), and even crime statistics do not allow reliable conclusions to be drawn about the relationship between rurality and criminality. Nevertheless, there are good reasons for concern. In many rural areas, where there are few alternative social centres, the pub is the focus of social interaction, especially for men, and after-hours late drinking is common in many areas. Social life for many rural people can become organised around drinking, and bingeing is often a feature of drinking patterns in situations where people's social contact is limited. In many market towns where there is all-day opening of pubs, and in small fishing villages and industrial villages, heavy prolonged drinking sessions are not uncommon. Furthermore, local drinking preferences, such as whisky drinking in Northern Ireland and Scotland, can also contribute to a greater risk of alcohol-related health and social problems.

As with other rural issues, there is often a reluctance to acknowledge that there is a problem, and consequently, an unwillingness to seek help when it is recognised. Alcohol Concern have found that the common practice in urban areas of providing alcohol and drug misuse services together in the same agency or location is counterproductive in rural areas, because it increases the stigma attached to seeking help (Alcohol Concern, 1996). The availability of alcohol services in rural areas is very variable, and access to appropriate help is something of a lottery depending upon where people live. Fortunately, several voluntary organisations have recognised these difficulties and there are a number of initiatives aimed at improving the situation. The National Council for Voluntary Organisations (NCVO) has highlighted the need for better information and has encouraged agencies to share their knowledge. Alcohol Concern has produced guidance on developing alcohol services in rural areas (Alcohol Concern, 1995), and also provides an excellent summary of planning and implementation points for new projects within its rural information pack (Alcohol Concern, 1996). Although alcohol problems are largely associated with men, with women and children being perceived as the victims of their drunken actions, there is a need for services to understand and respond to women's misuse too. Preston, in a general study (1996), of this aspect of alcohol misuse has attempted to identify why women do not use existing services and has made several recommendations which are relevant to rural areas.

Rural Stress and Suicide

Over the last ten years there has been increasing concern about the levels of stress and the risks of suicide among rural dwellers. In particular, the situation of farmers has been a focus of attention and there have been a number of initiatives which have sought to provide information and develop support for those at risk of stress and suicide. Farmers as an occupational group have long been recognised as having an increased risk of suicide, and this was often seen as being linked to their comparative isolation and the 'efficiency' with which they were able to attempt to kill themselves because of their access to guns and toxic chemicals, together with the reduced likelihood of them being discovered when they made suicide attempts by hanging or self-poisoning. Latterly, the intrinsically stressful nature of an occupation in which so many factors are not easily amenable to personal control, e.g. the weather, market prices and so on, has worsened as incomes have fallen on many small farms, and considerable instability has resulted from reductions in agricultural subsidies and from the BSE crisis which have eroded markets and confidence in the future. For example, the Royal Agricultural Benevolent Institution, a charity that provides advice and financial assistance to farmers found that calls for help increased tenfold during 1998. Increased awareness that there is a problem has been helped by the backing of the various national farmers' unions and the coverage given by rural media.

A study by Hawton et al. (1998), found relatively high suicide rates in Cambridgeshire, Devon, Hampshire, Humberside, Powys, Suffolk, Warwickshire, West Sussex, and West Yorkshire, and indicated that the increased risk arose from mental health problems exacerbated by occupational, financial, health, or relationship problems. It also found that the lack of social supports for farmers was a significant factor in their increased vulnerability to stress and suicide and recommended nation-wide initiatives to improve networks of support with special efforts directed towards high risk areas and high risk farmers. It is clear that the general social and economic circumstances of farmers, together with other factors, such as the general reluctance of men to seek help with mental health problems and the traditional value placed upon self-reliance in rural communities, makes farmers more vulnerable to self-harm. These cultural obstacles to seeking help require considerable shifts in attitudes from some of those towards whom such help is directed, and it is unlikely that significant changes will take place in the short term. It might be that such changes are better induced by embedding messages about stress within wider campaigns aimed at getting men, and especially working class men, to use medical services anyway. The Rural Stress Information Network is a useful source of information throughout the UK and they maintain a database of organisations and individuals offering help to farmers and act as a linking organisation between those who need help and those who may provide it. The Farm Crisis Network provides a national help line staffed by volunteers which is accessible through a single number charged at local rates.

It would be mistaken, however, to assume that the risk of rural suicide is only an issue for farmers. Many of the factors which contribute to their increased levels of risk, such as stress and social isolation, are also present for other people and occupations in the countryside. In fact, the Office for National Statistic's listing of proportional mortality ratios (1998), shows veterinarians, along with farmers, horticulturists and farm managers as the riskiest occupational group. Other rural occupations which seem to have an above average risk of suicide are forestry workers, groundsmen (sic) and gardeners, and other general occupations which also have higher risks include dentists, general practitioners, pharmacists, sales representatives and garage proprietors. The crucial point is that regardless of a person's age, sex or occupation, social workers should not let the myth of the rural idyll obscure the difficulties that some people face in making their problems known and in seeking appropriate help. The relative social isolation of some people and the widespread emphasis upon being independent, self-reliant and 'able to cope', makes it possible for some people at risk in the countryside to go unrecognised, when in other locations the signs of their distress might be more readily apparent. Men continue to have higher risk rates than women, though there are some indications of change which appear to be linked to the extent to which people live with others:

Divorced and widowed men continue to have the highest suicide rates although they have been declining since 1983. Suicide rates for single men have been increasing continuously since 1983 . . . (while) rates have been decreasing for all women . . . except for those who are single.

(ONS, 1998, p92)

Consequently, people who live alone and who lack emotional and social support from other people still continue to be among the most vulnerable to suicide. One other contributory factor which seems to be significant, especially in the deaths of younger people, is alcohol and drug misuse.

Conclusion

Unfortunately, the constraints of space has meant that some relevant issues, such as anti-poverty initiatives and joint work with health services, have not been addressed in this book, or have received only passing mention. There have been some difficult choices about what to include and what leave out, but the main themes of the book should be applicable to most aspects of rural services. The complexity of the rural context combined with the complexity of each person's individual social location means that there are few simple solutions to the task of meeting the multiplicity of problems and needs. Many of the studies and projects reviewed in this book demonstrate that creativity and flexibility are essential qualities when attempting to devise and deliver responsive services in what is often a very challenging environment. Nonetheless, some common themes have emerged from the discussion of rather different aspects of social service.

Good knowledge of the community and how it works is a prerequisite of success. Without an awareness of local dynamics and the personal politics of an area, workers will struggle to understand how people experience their problems. They will find difficulty in judging what sorts of response are likely to regarded as appropriate, which modes of intervention will bring the best results, and how best to mobilise the support and the informal resources of the local community, should they require it. Understanding some of the reasons which make people reluctant to approach and use services, can help workers to become much more sensitive to their concerns in regard to confidentiality, shame and stigma. These are considerable obstacles to be surmounted or circumvented, and they require that workers comprehend the practical difference between anonymity, which in urban areas is virtually assured by the size of the community, and confidentiality, which in a small rural community might be imperilled in some unexpected ways. It requires workers to become very skilled in negotiating the expectations and the pitfalls of rural social conventions, and in doing so, find ways of dealing with the fact that their own practice and personal life are much more exposed to the public gaze than would be the case in a city. In an urban area, the credibility of a worker is often established afresh in each new encounter with a client, for it is likely that neither party will have met or heard of each other before. However, in a rural area, reputations often precede first meetings and personal and professional credibility is usually a more public attainment or quality. Indeed, bad news does travel fast, and mistakes which reflect unfavourably upon workers, can take a very long time to recover from. The corollary, however, is that a pre-existing reputation of credibility can be a very effective resource when meeting people for the first time, or when seeking to persuade others to intervene or act in some other way.

Public lack of knowledge about services and low expectations are commonplace, and publicity and public education are crucial aspects of service provision in any setting, but word of mouth can be extraordinarily effective in rural areas when the area of service is one that people are willing to discuss with each other. Knowledge of a new dial-a-ride transport scheme or a nursery may spread quickly throughout a community, whereas services to people with sexually transmitted diseases or any other problems perceived as 'discreditable' are much less likely to circulate informally, where even the act of seeking help will be seen as risky. Existing organisations and networks often provide a valuable carrier of information about new developments, particularly since they tend to engage with those people who are most active in their local communities. They can provide excellent opportunities to explain why a service is needed and through enhancing understanding can accelerate the acceptance of innovative schemes, as well as promoting their take-up.

While community support is vital to the success of new services and the active engagement of people who are respected in their communities can do much to sustain projects, especially when there are personnel changes, the assumption that services can be developed with initial professional support and then continue without paid project workers, is rarely justified. Apart from the question of whether volunteers are available, and willing and able to shoulder a workload that was formerly undertaken by a paid worker, most local people have their own history which can make it difficult for them to adopt, and gain acceptance in, a new role. Similarly, although attempts to meet local needs and reduce transport time and costs by using locally recruited paid workers can be helpful in providing much-needed services, there are drawbacks. Sometimes these workers will 'not always be acceptable to those service users who . . . (are) concerned about confidentiality or . . . (are) reluctant to have service, especially intimate service, from neighbours whom they . . . (have) known for many years' (SSI, 1999, p10).

Understanding and dealing with social difference, whether it arises from age, gender, sexuality, class, mental capacity, ethnicity or other base, is

References

Acton, T. and Mundy, G. (1997) *Romani Culture and Gypsy Identity*, Hatfield, University of Hertfordshire Press.

Age Concern (1998) *Developing Rural Services to Older People*, London, Age Concern.

Ageyman, J. (1995) Environment, Heritage and Multiculturalism, *Interpretation: A Journal of Heritage and Environmental Interpretation*, pp5–6.

Ageyman, J. (1989) Black People, White Landscape, *Town and Country Planning*, December, 58, 12, pp336–8.

Ageyman, J. and Spooner, R. (1997) Ethnicity and the Rural Environment, in Cloke, P. and Little, J. (Eds.) *Contested Countryside Cultures: Otherness, Marginalisation and Rurality*, London, Routledge.

Alcock, P., Harrow, J., Macmillan, R., Vincent, J. and Pearson, S. (1999a) *Voluntary Sector Organisations Experiences of Funding*, Rowntree Research Findings, 149, http://www.jrf.org.uk

Alcock, P., Harrow, J., Macmillan, R., Vincent, J. and Pearson, S. (1999b) *Making Funding Work: Funding Regimes and Local Voluntary Organisations*, York, Rowntree Foundation.

Alcohol Concern (1995) *Developing Alcohol Services for Rural Areas*, London, Alcohol Concern.

Alcohol Concern (1996) *Rural Information Pack*, London, Alcohol Concern.

Aldridge, M. (1996) Dragged to Market: Being a Professional in a Postmodern World, *British Journal of Social Work*, 26, 2, pp177–94.

All Party Group on Alcohol Misuse (1995) *Alcohol and Crime: Breaking the Link*, London, Alcohol Concern.

Ashton, S. (1994) The Farmer Needs a Wife: Farm Women in Wales, in Aaron, J., Rees, T., Betts, S. and Vincentelli, M. (Eds.) *Our Sister's Land: The Changing Identities of Women in Wales*, University of Wales Press, Cardiff.

Audit Commission (2000) *Getting the Best from Social Services; News Release*, http://www.audit-commission.gov.uk

Barnes, L. (1993) *Getting Closer to Rural Communities*, London, NCVO.

Beresford, P. and Croft, S. (1993) *Citizen Involvement: A Practical Guide for Change*, London, Macmillan.

Berlan, M. (1988) The Division of Labour and Decision Making in Farming Couples: Power and Negotiation, *Sociologica Ruralis*, 28, 4.

Berry, B. J. L. (1976) *Urbanisation and Counterurbanisation*, Beverly Hills, California, Sage.

Bibby, P. (1994) *Personal Safety for Social Workers*, Aldershot, Arena.

Biehal, N., Clayden, J., Stein, M. and Wade, J. (1995) *Moving On: Young People and Leaving Care Schemes*, London, HMSO.

Bowie, F. (1993) Wales from Within: Conflicting Interpretations of Welsh Identity, in MacDonald, S. (Ed.) *Inside European Identities*, Berg, Oxford.

Bourdieu, P. (1984) *Distinction: A Social Critique of the Judgement of Taste*, Cambridge, Massachussets, Harvard University Press.

Boushel, M. (1994) The Protective Environment of Children: Towards a Framework for Anti-oppressive, Cross-cultural and Cross-national Understanding, *British Journal of Social* Work, 24, pp173–90.

Braye, S. and Preston-Shoot, M. (1995) *Empowering Practice in Social Care*, Buckingham, Open University Press.

Broad, B. (1999) Improving the Health of Children and Young People Leaving Care, *Adoption and Fostering*, 23, 1, pp40–8.

Brown, H. and Smith, H. (1993) Women Caring for People: the Mismatch Between Rhetoric and Women's Reality?, *Policy and Politics*, 21, 3, pp185–93.

Brown, R., Bute, S. and Ford, P. (1986) *Social Workers at Risk*, Macmillan, London.

Buchanan, J. (1983) *The Mobility of Disabled People in a Rural Environment*, London, Royal Association for Disability and Rehabilitation.

Burnett, K. A. (1996) Once an Incomer, Always an Incomer?, in Chapman, P., Burnett, K. A., McKie, L., Nelson, J., Bain, M., Raitt, F. and Lloyd, S. (Eds.) Aldershot, Avebury.

Butler, R. (1998) Rural Recreation and Tourism, in Ilbery, B. (Ed.) *The Geography of Rural Change*, Harlow, Addison Wesley Longman.

Cashmore, E. and Troyna, B. (1986) *An Introduction to Race Relations*, London, Routledge and Kegan Paul.

Cemlyn, S. (1999) On the Road to Understanding, *Community Care*, 12–18 August, pp24–5.

Cemlyn, S. (2000) Assimilation, control, Mediation or Advocacy? Social Work Dilemmas in Providing Anti-oppressive Services for Traveller Children and Families, *Child and Family Social Work*, in press.

Champion, A. (1989) *Counterurbanisation*, London, Edward Arnold.

Champion, T. and Watkins, C. (Eds.) (1991) *People in the Countryside*, London, Paul Chapman Publishing.

References

Chapman, P. (1996) Women's Experience of Rural Disadvantage, in Chapman, P. and Lloyd, S. (Eds.) *Women and Access in Rural Areas*, Aldershot, Avebury.

Ching, B. and Creed, G. (1997) *Knowing Your Place: Rural Identity and Cultural Hierarchy*, London, Routledge.

Clark, H., Dyer, S. and Horwood, J. (1998a) *'That Bit of Help'*: The High Value of Low Level Preventative Services for Older People, London, The Policy Press.

Clark, H., Dyer, S. and Horwood, J. (1998b) *The Importance of 'Low Level' Preventive Services to Older People*, Rowntree Research Findings, 768, http://www.jrf.org.uk

Cloke, P. (1997) Poor Country: Marginalisation, Poverty and Rurality, in Cloke, P. and Little, J. (Eds.) *Contested Countryside Cultures: Otherness, Marginalisation and Rurality*, Routledge, London.

Cloke, P., Goodwin, M. and Milbourne, P. (1997) *Rural Wales: Community and Marginalisation*, University of Wales Press, Cardiff.

Cloke, P., Goodwin, M., Milbourne, P. and Thomas, C. (1995) Deprivation, Poverty and Marginalisation in Rural Lifestyles in England and Wales, *Journal of Rural Studies*, 11, pp351–66

Cloke, P. and Little, J. (Eds.) (1997) *Contested Countryside Cultures: Otherness, Marginalisation and Rurality*, Routledge, London.

Cloke, P., Milbourne, P. and Thomas, C. (1994) *Lifestyles in Rural England*, London, Rural Development Commission.

Coates, I. (1993) A Cuckoo in the Nest: The National Front and Green Ideology, in Holder, J., Lane, P., Eden, S., Reeve, R., Collier, U. and Anderson, K. (Eds.) *Perspectives on the Environment: Interdisciplinary Research Network on the Environment and Society*, Aldershot, Avebury.

Cohen, B. (1995) *Childcare Services for Rural Families: Improving Provision in the European Union*, Brussels, Commission of the European Communities.

Cohen, B. (1995) Meeting the Needs of Rural Children: A European Perspective, in *Country Children Count*, ACC Publication London, pp9–14.

Cook, E. (1999) The Farmer of the Future, *The Independent on Sunday*, 29 August, p15.

Cox, F. M., Erlich, J. L., Rothman, J. and Tropman, J. E. (1987) *Strategies of Community Organization*, Itasca, Illinois, F. E. Peacock.

Craig, G., Ahmed, B. and Amery, F. (1999) 'We Shoot them at Newark': The Work of the Lincolnshire Forum for Racial Justice, in Henderson, P. and Kaur, R. (Eds.) *Rural Racism in the UK*, London, The Community Development Foundation.

Craig, G. and Manthorpe, J. (1999) *The Impact of Local Government Reorganisation on Social Work*, Rowntree Research Findings, 999, http://www.jrf.org.uk

Dalrymple, J. and Burke, B. (1995) *Anti-oppressive Practice: Social Care and the Law*, Buckingham, Open University Press.

Davidoff, L., L'Esperance, J. and Newby, H. (1976) Landscapes with Figures: Home and Community in English Society, in Mitchell, J. and Oakley, A. (Eds.) *The Rights and Wrongs of Women*, Harmondsworth, Penguin.

Davis, P. (1999) No Fear, *Community Care*, 30 September.

Denham, C. and White, I. (1998) Differences in Urban and Rural Britain, *Population Trends*, London, Office for National Statistics.

de Lima, P. (1999) Research and action in the Scottish Highlands, in Henderson, P. and Kaur, R. (Eds.) *Rural Racism in the UK*, London, The Community Development Foundation.

Department of Health (1996) *Developing Health and Social Care in Rural England*, London, Stationery Office.

Department of Health (1997) *Taking Care: Taking Control*, Social Services Inspectorate, London, Stationery Office.

DePoy, E. and Butler, S. (1996) Health: Elderly Rural Women's Conceptions, *Affilia*, 11, 2, pp207–20.

DETR (1998) *Modern Local Government: In Touch with the People*, Department of the Environment, Transport and the Regions, http://www.detr.gov.uk

DETR (2000) *Neighbourhood Statistics to Show True Scale of Deprivation*, News Release, http://press.detr.gov.uk

Dhalech, M. (1999) *Challenging Racism in the Rural Idyll, The Rural Race Equality Project*, Exeter.

Dhalech, M. (1999) Race Equality Initiatives in South West England, in Henderson, P. and Kaur, R. (Eds.) *Rural Racism in the UK*, The Community Development Foundation, London.

Dobash, R. P., Dobash, R. E., Wilson, M. and Daly, M. (1992) The Myth of Sexual Symmetry in Marital Violence, *Social Problems*, 39, 1, pp71–91.

Duncan, T. (1996) *Neighbours' Views of Official Sites for Travelling People*, Glasgow, The Planning Exchange.

Eaton, S. (1995) *Multi-agency Work with Young People in Difficulty*, Rowntree Research Findings, Social Care Research 68, http://www.jrf.org.uk

Edleson, J. L. and Frank, M. D. (1991) Rural Interventions in Woman Battering: One State's Strategies, *Families in Society: The Journal of Contemporary Human Services*, November, pp543–51.

Edwards, B., Goodwin, M., Pemberton, S. and Woods, M. (1999) *Partnership Working in Rural Regeneration*, Rowntree Research Findings, 039, http://www.jrf.org.uk

Eldon Lee, C. (1999) Trials and Joys in a Family of Eleven, *Shrewsbury Chronicle*, 21 October, p24.

Ellen Walsh, M. (1989) Rural Social Work Practice, in Compton, B. and Galaway, B. (Eds.) *Social Work Processes*, Pacific Grove, California, Brooks/ Cole Publishing.

Esslemont, E. and Harrington, J. (1991) *Swings and Roundabouts: The Highs and Lows of Life for Pre-school Children and their Families in Rural Powys*, Cardiff, Save the Children.

Fabes, R., Worsley, L. and Howard, M. (1983) *The Myth of the Rural Idyll*, Child Poverty Leicester, Action Group.

Fineman, S. (1985) *Social Work Stress and Intervention*, Aldershot, Gower.

Fisher, C. (1997) I Bought my First Saw with my Maternity Benefit, in Cloke, P. and Little, J. (Eds.) *Contested Countryside Cultures: Otherness, Marginalisation and Rurality*, London, Routledge.

Francis, D. and Henderson, P. (1992) *Working with Rural Communities*, London, Macmillan.

Fraser, A. (1995) *The Gypsies*, Oxford, Blackwell.

Fryer, P. (1984) *Staying Power: The History of Black People in Britain*, London, Pluto Press.

Furuseth, O. (1998) Service Provision and Social Deprivation, in Ilbery, B. (Ed.) *The Geography of Rural Change*, Harlow, Addison Wesley Longman.

Gant, R and Smith, J. (1991) The Elderly and the Disabled in Rural Areas: Travel Patterns in the North Cotswolds, in Champion, T. and Watkins, C. (Eds.) *People in the Countryside*, London, Paul Chapman Publishing.

Gibson, F., Whittington, D., Pattenden, A., Rahmin, L. and James, D. (1995) *Day Care in Rural Areas*, Rowntree Research Findings, Social Care Research 72, http://www.jrf.org.uk

Giddens, A. (1978) *Durkheim*, London, Fontana.

Giddens, A. (1984) *The Constitution of Society*, Cambridge, Polity Press.

Giddens, A. (1991) *Modernity and Self-identity: Self and Society in the Late Modern Age*, Cambridge, Polity Press.

Gieve, K. (Ed.) (1989) *Balancing Acts: On Becoming a Mother*, London, Virago.

Ginnety, P. (1993) *The Health of Travellers*, Belfast, Eastern Health and Social Services Board.

Gunner, J. (1999) *Home or Away?: Tackling Youth Homelessness in the Countryside*, London, Centrepoint and The Countryside Agency.

Hague, G., Malos, E. and Dear, W. (1996) *Multiagency Work and Domestic Violence: A National Study of Interagency Initiatives*, Bristol, The Policy Press.

Hague, G. (1999) Smoke Screen or Leap Forward: Interagency Initiatives as a Response to Domestic Violence, *Critical Social Policy*, 53, pp93–109.

Hague, G. (2000) *Reducing Domestic Violence ... What Works? MultiAgency Fora*, London, Home Office Research and Development and Statistics Directorate.

Hague, G. and Malos, E. (1996) *Tackling Domestic Violence: A Guide to Developing Multiagency Initiatives*, Bristol, The Policy Press.

Halfacree, K. (1993) Locality and Social Representation: Space Discourse and Alternative Definitions of the Rural, *Journal of Rural Studies*, 9, pp23–7

Halfacree, K. (1997) Contrasting Roles for the Post-productivist Countryside, in Cloke, P. and Little, J. (Eds.) (1997) *Contested Countryside Cultures: Otherness, Marginalisation and Rurality*, London, Routledge.

Harper, S. (1991) People Moving to the Countryside: Case Studies of Decision Making, in Champion, T. and Watkins, C. (Eds.) *People in the Countryside*, London, Paul Chapman Publishing.

Hawes, D. and Perez, B. (1996) *The Gypsy and the State: The Ethnic Cleansing of British Society*, Bristol, The Policy Press.

Hawkins, P. and Shohet, R. (1989) *Supervision in the Helping Professions*, Buckingham, Open University Press.

Hawton, K., Simkin, S., Malmberg, A., Fagg, J. and Harriss, L. (1998) *Suicide and Stress in Farmers*, London, Department of Health.

Hayle, R. (1996) *Fair Shares for Rural Areas? An Assessment of Public Resource Allocation Systems*, London, Rural Development Commission.

Help the Aged (1996) *Growing Old in the Countryside*, London, Help the Aged/Rural Development Commission.

Henderson, S. (1998) *Drugs Prevention in Rural Areas: An Evaluation Report*, London, HMSO, Paper 17.

Henderson, S. (2000) Sticks and Smoke: Country Cousins and Close Communities, *Drug Link*, pp12–5, January/February.

Henderson, P. and Kaur, R. (1999) *Rural Racism in the UK*, London, The Community Development Foundation.

Hetherington, K. (1995) *On the Homecoming of the Stranger: New Social Movements or New Sociations?*, Lancaster Regionalism Group, Working Paper 39, University of Lancaster.

Hetherington, P. (1999) 'Allow More Building on Farmland', Prescott Told, *The Guardian*, 21 October, p6.

Hirst, J. (1999) Pulled Every Which Way, *Community Care*, 19–25 August.

HMSO (1997) Annual Abstract of Statistics, London, HMSO.

HMSO (1999) Annual Abstract of Statistics, London, HMSO.

HMSO (1999) *Explanatory Notes to the Local Government Act*, http://www.hmso.gov.uk

Home Office (2000) *Reducing Domestic Violence: What Works*, London, Home Office Research and Development and Statistics Directorate.

Hooper, C.A. (1996) *Evaluation of a Self-Help Support Project for Rural Lone Parents*, Rowntree Research Findings, Social Policy Research 108, http://www.jrf.org.uk

References

Hooyman, N. and Gonyea, J. (1995) *Feminist Perspectives on Family Care: Policies for Gender Justice*, London, Sage.

Hughes, A. (1997) Reality and 'Cultures of Womanhood' in Cloke, P. and Little, J. (Eds.) *Contested Countryside Cultures: Otherness, Marginalisation and Rurality* (1997) London, Routledge.

Ilbery, B. (1998) *The Geography of Rural Change*, Harlow, Addison Wesley Longman.

Jay, E. (1992) *Keep Them in Birmingham: Challenging Racism in the South West*, London, Commission for Racial Equality.

Jones, O. (1997) Little Figures, Big Shadows: Country Childhood Stories, in Cloke, P. and Little, J. (Eds.) *Contested Countryside Cultures: Otherness, Marginalisation and Rurality* (1997), London, Routledge.

Jordan, B. (1997) Service Users' Involvement in Child Protection and Family Support, in Parton, N. (Ed.) *Child Protection and Family Support*, London, Routledge.

Joseph Rowntree Foundation (1998) *Poverty and Exclusion in Rural Britain: The Dynamics of Low Income and Employment*, Bulletin 418, York.

Kadushin, A. (1976) *Supervision in Social Work*, New York, Columbia University Press.

Kelly, L. (2000) *Reducing Domestic Violence . . . What Works? Outreach and Advocacy Approaches*, London, Home Office Research and Development and Statistics Directorate.

Leitner, M. and Shapland, J. (1996) *Urban/Rural Variation in Drug Use and Attitudes Towards Drugs Prevention*, unpublished report to the Home Office Drugs Prevention Initiative.

Lewis, G. (1998) Rural Migration and Demographic Change, in Ilbery, B. (Ed.) *The Geography of Rural Change*, Harlow, Addison Wesley Longman.

Lewis, G. and Sherwood, K. (1994) *Rural Mobility and Housing*, Working Papers 7–11, Department of Geography, University of Leicester.

Lindow, V. (1999) *Evaluation of the National User Involvement Project*, Rowntree Research Findings, 129, http://www.jrf.org.uk

Little, J. (1987) Gender Relations in Rural Areas: The Importance of Women's Domestic Role, *Journal of Rural Studies*, 3, 4, pp335–42.

Little, J. (1997) Employment, Marginality and Women's Self-identity, in Cloke, P. and Little, J. (Eds.) *Contested Countryside Cultures: Otherness, Marginalisation and Rurality* (1997), London, Routledge.

Lowe, P., Bradley, T. and Wright, S. (Eds.) (1986) *Deprivation and Welfare in Rural Areas*, Norwich, Geobooks.

Lucas, J. (1992) Piece of Mind, *Social Work Today*, 10 November, pp14–5.

MacKay, A. (2000) *Reaching Out: Women's Aid in a Rural Area*, St. Andrews, East Fife Women's Aid.

MacLaughlin, B. (1986) The Rhetoric and Reality of Rural Deprivation, *Journal of Rural Studies* 2, 4, pp291–307.

MAFF (1989) *Agricultural Statistics for the United Kingdom 1987*, Ministry of Agriculture, Fisheries and Food, Department of Agriculture and Fisheries for Scotland, Department of Agriculture and Fisheries for Northern Ireland, Welsh Office, London, HMSO.

Manning, C. and Cheers, B. (1995) Child Abuse Notification in a Country Town, *Child Abuse and Neglect*, 19, 4, pp387–97.

Martinez-Brawley, E. (1982) *Rural Social and Community Work in the US and Britain*, New York, Praeger.

Martinez-Brawley, E. (1986) Community-oriented Social Work in a Rural and Remote Hebridean Patch, *International Social Work*, 29, pp349–72.

Martinez-Brawley, E. (1991) Social Services in Spain: The Case of Rural Catalonia, *International Social Work*, 34, pp265–86

Mason, D. (1995) *Race and Ethnicity in Modern Britain*, Oxford, Oxford University Press.

Mason, S. and Taylor, R. (1990) *Tackling Deprivation in Rural Areas: Effective Use of Charity Funding*, Cirencester, Gloucestershire, ACRE.

Marx, K. and Engels, F. (1972) *Manifesto of the Communist Party*, Foreign Languages Press, Peking, China.

Midgley, G., Munro, I. and Brown, M. (1997) *Integrating User Involvement and Multi-agency Working to Improve Housing for Older People*, Rowntree Research Findings, Housing Research 205, http://www.jrf.org.uk

Mirlees-Black, C. (1999) *Domestic Violence: Findings from a New British Crime Survey Self-completion Questionnaire*, London, Home Office Research Study, 191.

Mitchell, D. (1998) Peak Practice, *Community Care*, 26 February–4 March, p26.

More, W. (1997) *A New ABC of Handling Violence and Aggression*, Birmingham, Pepar Publications.

Morris, J. (1994) *The Shape of Things to Come? User-Led Social Services*, National Institute for Social Work, Social Services Policy Forum Paper No. 3.

Morrison, T. (1993) *Supervision in Social Care*, London, Longman.

Moseley, M. (1997) Parish Appraisals as a Tool of Rural Community Development: An Assessment of the British Experience, *Planning Practice and Research*, 12, 3, pp197–212.

Mullender, A. (1996) *Rethinking Domestic Violence: The Social Work and Probation Response*, London, Routledge.

Mullender, A. (2000) *Rethinking Domestic Violence . . . What Works? Meeting the Needs of Children*, London, Home Office Research and Development and Statistics Directorate.

Munro, I. S. (1978) In Preface, *The Country Child*, Centre for the Study of Rural Society, Lincoln.

References

Murdoch, J. and Pratt, A. C. (1997) From the Power of Topography to the Topography of Power, in Cloke, P. and Little, J. (Eds.) *Contested Countryside Cultures: Otherness, Marginalisation and Rurality* (1997) London, Routledge.

Murdoch, J. and Marsden, T. (1994) *Reconstituting Rurality*, London, UCL Press.

Myers, P. (1995) Country Mutters, *The Guardian*, March 21, pp4–5.

National Children's Play and Recreation Unit (1992) *Children Today in Devon: Playing in the Countryside—A study of Rural Children's Services*, London, National Children's Play and Recreation Unit.

NCVO (1994) *Not Just Fine Tuning*, London, National Council for Voluntary Organisations.

NCVO (1994) *Counting the Rural Cost: The Case for a Rural Premium in Voluntary Sector Funding*, London, National Council for Voluntary Organisations.

Newby, H. (1988) *The Countryside in Question*, London, Hutchinson.

NFWI (1993) *Caring for Rural Carers*, London, National Federation of Women's Institutes.

NFWI (1999) *The Changing Village*, London, National Federation of Women's Institutes.

Nizhar, P. (1995) *No Problem? Race Issues in Shropshire*, London, CRE.

Norris, D. (1990) *Violence Against Social Workers*, London, Kingsley.

North, D. (1998) Rural Industrialisation, in Ilbery, B. (Ed.) *The Geography of Rural Change*, Harlow, Addison Wesley Longman.

Office of Population Censuses and Surveys (1992) Census 1991, London, HMSO.

Office for National Statistics (1997) *Population Trends*, 88, Summer, pp27–8.

Office for National Statistics (1998) *Population Trends*, 92, Summer, pp33–41.

Okely, J. (1997) Non-territorial Culture as the Rationale for the Assimilation of Gypsy Children, *Childhood: A Global Journal of Child Research*, 4, 1, pp63–80.

Oliver, M. (1996) *Understanding Disability: From Theory to Practice*, London, Macmillan.

Palmer, J. (1991) *Children in Rural Communities: Scotland in Europe*, Edinburgh, HMSO.

Perkin, H. (1969) *The Origins of Modern English Society 1780–1880*, London, Routledge and Kegan Paul.

Peters, M. (1997) Social Exclusion, in Lavery, G., Pender, J. and Peters, M. (Eds.) *Exclusion and Inclusion: Minorities in Europe*, Leeds, Leeds Metropolitan university, ISPRU Occasional Papers in Social Studies.

Phillips, M. (1998) Social Perspectives, in Ilbery, B. (Ed.) *The Geography of Rural Change*, Harlow, Addison Wesley Longman.

Pizey, N. and Lyon, R. (1998) *Developing Rural Services to Older People*, London, Age Concern.

Powys Partnership Project (1996) *Powys Partnership Project Evaluation*, Llandrindod Wells, Powys County Council.

Poyner, B. and Warne, C. (1986) *Violence to Staff: A Basis for Assessment and Prevention*, London, HMSO.

Preston, L. (1996) *Women and Alcohol: Defining the Problem and Seeking Help*, Norwich, University of East Anglia, NORCAS.

Pugh, (1996) *Effective Language in Health and Social Work*, London, Chapman and Hall.

Pugh, R. (1997a) Change in British Social Work: The Lure of Post-modernism and its Pessimistic Conclusions, in Lesnik, B. (Ed.) *Change in Social Work*, Aldershot, Arena.

Pugh, R. (1997b) Considering Social Difference, in Bates, J., Pugh, R. and Thompson, N. (Eds.) *Child Protection: Challenges and Change*, Aldershot, Arena.

Pugh, R. (1997c) The Management of Violence and Aggressive Behaviour, in *Fundamentals of Social Care*, Prospect Publications.

Pugh, R. (1998) Language, Access and Identity, *Care: The Journal of Practice and Development*, 7, 1, pp14–26.

Pugh, R. and Gould, N. (2000) Globalisation, Social Work and Social Welfare, *European Journal of Social Work*, 2, 8:2 pp123–38.

Pugh, R. and Richards, M. (1996) Speaking Out: A Practical Approach to Empowerment, *Practice*, 8, 2, pp35–44.

Pugh, R. and Thompson, N. (1999) Social Work, Citizenship, and Constitutional Change, in Lesnik, B. (Ed.) *Social Work and the State: International Perspectives in Social Work*, Brighton, Pavilion.

Rapport, N. (1993) *Diverse World Views in an English Village*, Edinburgh, Edinburgh University Press.

Rickford, F. (1995) Country Living, *Community Care*, 19–25 October, pp14–5.

Rickford, F. (1996) Country Myths, *Community Care*, 25–31 July, p26.

Robinson, G. M. (1998) *Conflict and Change in the Countryside*, Chichester, John Wiley and Sons.

Ronnsby, A. (1994) *Mobilising Local Communities*, Ostersund, Mid-Sweden University.

Rugg, J. and Jones, A. (1999) Housing and Employment Problems for Young People in the Countryside, Rowntree Research Findings, N59, http://www.jrf.org.uk

Rural Development Commission (1998) *Local Authority Social Services in Rural Areas*, London, Rural Development Commission.

Russell, A. (1975) *The Village in Myth and Reality*, London, Chester House Publications.

Savigear, E. (1996) *The Servant Church: Organising Rural Community Care*, Stoneleigh Park, Acora Publishing.

Schama, S. (1995) *Landscape and Memory*, London, Harper Collins.

Seenan, G. (1999) Highland Retreat, *The Guardian*, October 28.

Shaw, M. (1979) *Rural Deprivation and Planning*, Norwich, Geobooks.

Short, B. (1992) *The English Rural Community: Image and Analysis*, Cambridge, Cambridge University Press.

Shropshire County Council (2000) *Reflecting Rural Issues: Implications for Performance Management*, Discussion Paper.

Shropshire Regeneration Partnership (1998) *Fairer Funding for Shropshire Public Services*, Shropshire County Council.

Shucksmith, M., Chapman, P., Clark, G., Black, S. and Conway, E. (1995) *Rural Scotland Today: The Best of Both Worlds?*, Edinburgh, HMSO.

Shucksmith, M. and Chapman, P. (1998) Rural Development and Social Exclusion, in *Sociologica Ruralis*, 28, 2, pp225–42.

Sibley, D. (1995) *Geographies of Exclusion: Society and Difference in the West*, London, Routledge.

Sibley, D. (1997) Endangering the Sacred: Nomads, Youth Cultures and the Countryside, in Cloke, P. and Little, J. (Eds.) *Contested Countryside Cultures: Otherness, Marginalisation and Rurality* (1997), London, Routledge.

Simons, R. L., Johnson, C., Conger, R. D. and Lorenz, F. O. (1997) Linking Community Context to Quality of Parenting: A Study of Rural Families, *Rural Sociology*, 62, 2, pp207–30.

Social Services Inspectorate (1988) *Social Services in a Multi-Racial Society*, London, Department of Health.

Social Services Inspectorate (1998a) *Inspection of Community Care Services in Rural Areas—Dorset County Council*, Bristol, Department of Health.

Social Services Inspectorate (1998b) *Inspection of Community Care Services in Rural Areas—Wiltshire County Council*, Bristol, Department of Health.

Social Services Inspectorate (1999) *Care in the Country—Inspection of Community Care Services in Rural Areas*, London, Department of Health.

Spilsbury, M. and Lloyd, N. (1998) *1997 Survey of Rural Service: A Report to the Rural Development Commission*, London, Rural Development Commission.

Statham, J. and Cameron, C. (1994) Young Children in Rural Areas: Implementing the Children Act, *Children and Society*, 8, 1.

Stein, M. (1991) *Leaving Care and the 1989 Children Act*, Leeds, First Key.

Stern, E. and Turbin, J. (1986) *Youth Employment and Unemployment in Rural England*, The Rural Development Commission, London.

Stewart, R. and Kilfeather, J. (1999) Working with Travellers in Northern Ireland, in Henderson, P. and Kaur, R. (Eds.) *Rural Racism in the UK*, London, The Community Development Foundation.

Stone, M. (1990) *Rural Childcare*, London, Rural Development Commission.
Taylor, I. (1999) She's There for me: Caring in a Rural Community, in Watson, S. and Doyal, L. (Eds.) *Engendering Social Policy*, Buckingham, Open University Press.
Townsend, P. (1979) *Poverty in the UK*, London, Allen Lane.
University of York (1998) *Population Distribution and Sparsity: Effects on Personal Social Services*, York, Centre for Health Economics.
Urry, J. (1995) A Middle Class Countryside?, in Butler, T. and Savage, M. (Eds.) *Social Change and the Middle Classes*, London, Routledge.
Vaughan, S. (1996) *Why Should Country Children Miss Out?/Pam Ddylai Plant y Wlad Golli Allan?*, Cardiff, Save the Children.
Walker, A. (Ed.) (1978) *Rural Poverty: Poverty, Deprivation and Planning in Rural Areas*, London, Child Poverty Action Group.
Warnes, T. and Ford, R. (1993) *The Changing Distribution of Elderly People: Great Britain 1981–1991*, Occasional paper No. 37, London, Department of Geography, Kings College.
Wenger, C. (1994) Old Women in Rural Wales: Variations in Adaptation, in Aaron, J., Rees, T., Betts, S. and Vincentelli, M. (Eds.) *Our Sister's Land: The Changing Identities of Women in Wales*, Cardiff, University of Wales Press.
Westwood, S. and Bhachu, P. (Eds.) (1988) *Enterprising Women: Ethnicity, Economy and Gender Relations*, London, Tavistock.
Whatmore, S. (1990) *Farming Women: Gender, Work and Family Enterprise*, London, Macmillan.
Whatmore, S. (1998) Theoretical Achievements and Challenges in European Rural Gender Studies, first published in *Rural Society*, 3, 4, and later published on the web by Charles Sturt University, Wagga Wagga, Australia, (www.csu.edu.au/research/crsr/ruralsoc/).
Whittle, K. (1995) Partnerships in Practice: Developments and Achievements, in *Country Children Count*, London, Association of County Councils.
Williams, C. (1997) 'Colour in the Pictures': A Welsh Guyanese Childhood, *Planet*, 125, pp25–30.
Williams, F. (1988) *Social Policy: A Critical Introduction*, Cambridge, Polity.
Woollett, S. (1993) *Counting the Cost: The Case for a Rural Premium*, London, National Council for Voluntary Organisations.
Yanay, U. (1989) Limits of Profesional Practice in Decentralized Systems, *Social Policy and Administration*, 23, 1, pp48–59.
Yelloly, M. and Henkel, M. (1995) *Learning and Teaching in Social Work: Towards Reflective Practice*, London.

Index

165